REDUCING NUCLEAR DANGER

REDUCING NUCLEAR DANGER

The Road Away from the Brink

McGeorge Bundy

William J. Crowe, Jr.

Sidney D. Drell

COUNCIL ON FOREIGN RELATIONS PRESS

NEW YORK

COUNCIL ON FOREIGN RELATIONS BOOKS

The Council on Foreign Relations, Inc., is a nonprofit and non-partisan organization devoted to promoting improved understanding of international affairs through the free exchange of ideas. The Council does not take any position on questions of foreign policy and has no affiliation with, and receives no funding from, the United States government.

From time to time, books and monographs written by members of the Council's research staff or visiting fellows, or commissioned by the Council, or written by an independent author with critical review contributed by a Council study or working group are published with the designation "Council on Foreign Relations Book." Any book or monograph bearing that designation is, in the judgment of the Committee on Studies of the Council's Board of Directors, a responsible treatment of a significant international topic worthy of presentation to the public. All statements of fact and expressions of opinion contained in Council books are, however, the sole responsibility of the author.

If you would like more information on Council publications, please write the Council on Foreign Relations, 58 East 68th Street, New York, NY 10021, or call the Publications Office at (212)734-0400.

Copyright © 1993 by the Council on Foreign Relations®, Inc.
All rights reserved.
Printed in the United States of America.

Library of Congress Cataloging-in-Publication Data

Bundy, McGeorge
    Reducing nuclear danger : the road away from the
brink / McGeorge Bundy, William J. Crowe, Jr., Sidney D. Drell.
    p. cm.
    Includes bibliographical references and index.
    ISBN 0-87609-149-4 : $14.95
    1. United States--Military policy. 2. Nuclear weapons--
United States. 3. Nuclear non-proliferation. 4. Nuclear arms
control. I. Crowe, William J., 1925- . II. Drell, Sidney D.
(Sidney David), 1926- . III. Title.

UA23.B7864 1993
355'.0335/73--dc20   93-35831
                         CIP

93 94 95 96 97 EB 10 9 8 7 6 5 4 3 2 1

Cover Design: Michael Storrings

Contents

Acknowledgments

This book is the product of a decision in 1990 by the Carnegie Corporation of New York to invite the three of us to work as co-chairmen of a Carnegie Commission on Reducing the Nuclear Danger. We have worked together now for more than two years, trying to understand a world of nuclear danger that has been changing month by month in ways that are astonishing both in magnitude and speed. The temptation all along has been to wait for further lessons from the next decisions of governments, and as we commit this report to press in June 1993 we are well aware that readers must assess it against what will have happened between now and the time of their reading.

We have tried to distinguish broad principles from interesting details, and in particular we have tried not to be parochial—not to argue just from our individual experience, whether political, military, or scientific. We have worked our way from individual to collective judgments on a wide variety of issues, and we believe the result is the better for that work. We write as Americans, but we have tried to take account of the reality that citizens of other countries think in their own ways.

It was the original hope of the Carnegie Corporation that this report could be the shared product of a larger number of students of this question, and a most distinguished group was recruited to this end. But as it turned out the three of us used most of the available time in hammering out our own agreed views. About half the fault lies in ourselves and the other half in the pace of events, which kept us busy changing our minds about what we really thought. Nonetheless we did get excellent counsel from many of those who originally agreed to help, as we did from an overlapping group of advisers assembled by the Council on Foreign Relations to consider our draft. We are grateful to all of the following, and none of them should be blamed for our mistakes: Harold Brown, Alton Frye, Andrew J. Goodpaster, David Haproff, Michael Krepon, Thomas K. Longstreth, Robert S. McNamara, Janne E. Nolan, Wolfgang K.H. Panofsky, John P. Rhinelander, Thomas C. Schelling, Gerard C. Smith, and Leonard S. Spector.

We have been greatly assisted by our professional adviser Michèle Flournoy, who has backed up our work by all sorts of help—checking and correcting our understanding of the past, keeping us alert to the best work—of the ablest younger scholars, of whom she is one, challenging many of our conclusions and changing some, and sharpening our argument by telling us what might not be understood by serious students if we did not explain ourselves better. We have also had indispensable help in the preparation, collation, circulation, and correction of drafts, and the management of meetings from Brooke Jaffe, Bonnie Rose, Adrianne Grunberg, and Georganne Brown.

Finally we must express our warmest personal thanks to Dr. David A. Hamburg, the president of the Carnegie Corporation. The enterprise was his idea, and his encouragement has helped us all along the way. The staff of the Carnegie Corporation has helped with unfailing kindness and understanding.

Introduction

NOW IS AN UNCOMMONLY GOOD TIME FOR AMERICANS to look again at an issue we have faced for more than fifty years: the problem of danger from nuclear warheads, a phrase that we shorten in this report to "nuclear danger." Of course there are other nuclear dangers, as from badly designed or badly managed power plants or from badly handled waste disposal, but the subject of this book is nuclear warheads—the most massive single threat to humanity. In this field the problems and opportunities of the years ahead are different from those of even a few years ago, and we must bring our national thinking up to date. Nuclear danger persists, inherent in what we know how to do, concrete in the warheads possessed by at least eight nations, present in the ambitions of others, and connected by fear and hope to the changing political relations of states both with and without nuclear weapons.

The end of the Cold War has greatly reduced the immediacy of the general nuclear fear that was a recurrent element of that long contest; Americans think about Russians very differently now and are right to do so. But it would be dangerously wrong to suppose that the end of the Cold War means an end of nuclear danger, and it would be a grave error for our people or our government to let nuclear fear be replaced by nuclear complacency. Indeed it is not at all clear that the overall *level* of nuclear danger has gone down.

But great events have drastically changed the *shape* of that danger, and also the shape of nuclear fear and hope. There is now a new chance for stable nuclear peace, especially, but not uniquely, between the United States and Russia. There is also a new chance for change in the behavior of all who are concerned with the spread of nuclear weapons into dangerous hands. But there are newly visible hazards both in the breakup of the old Soviet Union and in the demonstrated weakness of international efforts to limit nuclear spread. In this new situation neither the imperatives nor the impossibles of past conventional wisdom will be a good basis for effective policy.

We should emphasize at the start that we do not have pat answers. The three of us have had long experience with nuclear danger, both as students of the problem and as participants in national decision-making. We came to these matters through the different avenues of scientific, military, and political experience, but all of us have learned that nuclear choices are never merely scientific, or military, or political. At least one of us has seen a thermonuclear test, taken part in a nuclear crisis, commanded nuclear forces, faced the nuclear questions of presidents, played in classified nuclear war games, negotiated with allies, and worked with representatives of the Soviet Union. We have learned from teachers as different as Henry L. Stimson, Andrei Sakharov, and Sergei Akhromeyev. We have worked on governmental assessments of both nuclear weapons systems and arms control agreements. We have also had opportunities for advanced study at universities as varied as Harvard, Illinois, Massachusetts Institute of Technology, New York University, Oklahoma, Princeton, and Stanford. We do not cite our experience to claim that it answers all questions, but rather to make it clear that the large changes of policy which we join in recommending are not produced *only* by the valor of ignorance. Yet in fact all students of this subject need such valor, because no one wants to learn about nuclear warfare from direct experience.

The nuclear issues of the post–Cold War world require the fresh and sustained attention of all who help in making the decisions of our country, and to us that means, at least potentially, all our fellow citizens. No magical understanding is conferred either by experience or by specialized knowledge, important as both can be. This report is an effort to contribute to a new process of national understanding which will need help from as many Americans as possible.

We write, first of all, as Americans, and for Americans, although we hope our analysis may be helpful also in the wider discussions that will be indispensable for effective international understanding and action. The problem of nuclear danger has no political boundary, and there is not much that American policy can achieve alone. A principal theme of this analysis is that the basic objective of American nuclear policy—a sustained and solid reduction of nuclear danger—cannot be achieved without the support of many countries, each with its own deeply cherished objectives and its own fiercely defended right to decide for itself. Nonetheless both history and present power give a special importance to what Americans do and do not decide. Without American skill and good sense the prospect of stable and sustained reduction in nuclear danger is unlikely to be realized at any level: not between Russians and Americans; not in the future behavior of other newly independent states of the former Soviet Union; not in the behavior of other nuclear-weapon states; and not in the complex process of international action to end or limit sharply the spread of nuclear weapons.

There has been a dramatic but unfinished change in the basic relationship between the United States and what we used to call the Soviet Union. The Cold War has ended, and so has the Soviet Union as we knew it for more than seventy years. With the exception of nuclear armament only one superpower remains, but the exception is crucial. In this situation there is a new nuclear danger, arising from uncertainty about who will control the nuclear weapons still deployed in several states of the former Soviet Union, but there is also a new practice of Russian-American cooperation in reducing the massive nuclear competition with which the two societies have lived since the 1940s. There is also a more familiar danger, now greatly reduced but not beyond revival, that Russian-American hostility could be renewed, for example after a political takeover by hardliners in Moscow.

The break-up of the Soviet Union and the escape of Eastern Europe from Soviet domination have produced a remarkable change in what the United States must ask of its own nuclear weapons. From the beginning of the Cold War to the end of 1989 the Soviets and their satellites were widely believed to possess in Europe a superiority in conventional weapons that could have been politically commanding without the presence of an American deterrent capability in nuclear weapons. The elimination of the longstanding conventional superiority of Soviet military power in Europe removed the only significant requirement that American nuclear weapons be available to prevent *conventional* defeat. American deterrent capability in Europe is now required only to balance Russian *nuclear* strength, since Russia plainly has neither the conventional strength nor the political will to march westward against the rest of Europe. This revolution in the conventional balance and in politics means that for the first time in the nuclear age the United States and its European friends would clearly be safe if there were no nuclear weapons on either side of the old Iron Curtain. Absent the requirement for a first-use capability in Europe, it becomes a general interest of Americans and their allies, as it was *not* in the Cold War decades, that the role of nuclear weapons should be reduced. This change in the fundamental strategic balance between Russia and the West has already permitted dramatic changes in American nuclear programs, plans, and arms control arrangements.

From the beginning of the Cold War in 1946 to its end in 1990, the U. S. government would have rejected any offer from the gods to take all nuclear weapons off the table of international affairs. Today such an offer would deserve instant acceptance; it would remove all kinds of risks of catastrophic destruction, and it would leave us and our friends quite safe from Russian expansion. We should be free to enjoy two extraordinary strategic advantages: first, as the least threatened of major states and second, as the one state with modern conventional forces of unmatched quality. Unfortunately no one knows how to abolish nuclear weapons, but the dramatic change in what we now need from these weapons makes a great difference in the limits we can accept on the size and use of our own nuclear forces, and that difference in turn affects what others can decide.

Saddam Hussein has provided a sharp reminder of a different nuclear danger—that nuclear weapons may come into the hands of unpredictable and adventurous rulers. We learned in Iraq that when international awareness, will, and capability are all three sufficient, it is possible to take effective action against such danger. This new knowledge of what is possible has created a new political opportunity for action that will prevent the emergence of such additional nuclear-weapon states, but it is not an opportunity that can be seized by any one or two nations unaccompanied by others. The case of Saddam is unique both in the breadth of the international judgment that a bomb under his control would be unacceptably dangerous and in the strength of the American presence and engagement created by his aggression against Kuwait. Multinational action against the Iraqi bomb has been effective, at least in the short run, but it should not mislead us into a judgment that all such cases will be easy.

THE STRUCTURE OF THIS BOOK

In the first chapter we consider the issues now before the Soviet Union's successor states and the United States. Dramatic reductions in strategic weapons have already been formally agreed in the START I and START II treaties, and there is agreement in principle that only Russia, among the successor states of the Soviet Union, will continue to have nuclear weapons, although large numbers of strategic warheads may remain outside Russia for years. Much remains to be done on this front, and while active American help has already proved its value, a still more energetic policy of cooperation is needed in support of currently agreed objectives: ensuring that Russia is a stable and moderate partner with the United States, as the two nuclear superpowers, and that the other successor states remain free from the costs and dangers of possessing nuclear weapons.

In the second chapter we address the much wider problem of limiting the spread of nuclear weapons around the world. The present alignment of nations is at once complex and promising. The problem of nuclear proliferation inevitably involves not only the would-be proliferators but also the many countries that could be their suppliers. It is particularly important to recognize that the world is not divided simply into countries that have nuclear weapons and countries that wish they had them. There are many who have happily stood aside from any such undertaking, and the countries that do have nuclear weapons have varied interests and attitudes. There is both need and support for a new level of international commitment to much stronger programs of action against the spread of nuclear danger.

In the third and final chapter we offer some general conclusions on the principles that should guide U.S. policy on this question in the years immediately ahead. There is now a good prospect that our approach to the former Soviet Union, our approach to proliferation, and the conduct of our national policy toward nuclear weapons can reinforce each other. This conclusion is important, because often in the past there has been conflict or the appearance of conflict between one American objective and another in nuclear matters.

The three chapters will elaborate a few general propositions that it may help to set out briefly at the start. First, fifty years of nuclear experience show that the nuclear weapon is indeed different from any other. It is different because even a single warhead can do enormous damage, both military and human, and because a country that can have one can have tens, or hundreds, or even tens of thousands—as do the United States and Russia today. Because of its unique destructiveness, this weapon has gone unused since Nagasaki in 1945. Every country with nuclear weapons has been at war, and most of them have been losers in war, but none has resorted to nuclear warheads. Moreover there is no significant school of thought, in any nuclear-weapon state, that argues that it would have been better to use the bomb than to accept this or that unsatisfactory result. For Americans the most notable case in which that argument is not publicly pressed by critics is Vietnam. After forty-eight years in which no one has attacked anyone with nuclear weapons, the world has a strong "tradition for their non-use."[1] The tradition of nonuse is now of such value that its preservation should be a goal of great importance for all states. For all countries, and especially for the United States, any first use of nuclear weapons should be truly a *defensive last resort*, never a matter of military discretion. There is now no vital interest of the United States, except the deterrence of *nuclear* attack, that cannot be met by prudent conventional readiness—there is no visible case where the United States could be forced to choose between defeat and the first use of nuclear weapons.

Second, we believe that there is no nuclear-weapon state today that cannot gain from a reduction of its current reliance on nuclear weapons, and no non-nuclear-weapon state today that can expect a net advantage in

---

[1]The phenomenon was first described, and the phrase invented, in 1960 by Thomas Schelling.

attempting to have such weapons of its own. This is not an abstract rule; it is an argument based on the present real condition of every country. In particular, the United States and the states of the former Soviet Union have a common interest in expanding and deepening their interlocking reductions of nuclear weaponry and their cooperative efforts to make such reductions visibly reliable to each other and the world. In due course a parallel reduction of reliance on nuclear weaponry will be advantageous to all other nuclear-weapon states. It is in the real interest of all countries that there should be no increase in the number of nuclear-weapon states, and we believe that it is possible for this common interest to prevail even in the face of the undesirable nuclear ambitions of a few leaders. Recent experience with nuclear danger in every part of the world has underlined the same decisive reality: increased reliance on nuclear weapons, because of the fearful reactions it stimulates, is in the true long-run interest of no country.

Third, the United States should give financial support to all its programs for reducing nuclear danger. A program that attends to U.S. nuclear reductions, strongly assists in the turn away from warheads by other countries, and reinforces the worldwide effort against proliferation will be much less expensive than the spending programs we have had during the long nuclear arms competition.

Such a program should begin with increased American support for the accelerated dismantling of Soviet nuclear weapons in Russia, Belarus, Kazakhstan, and Ukraine. Although the latter three have formally agreed to renounce nuclear weapons, much remains to be done to make this agreement a reality. Thousands of strategic nuclear warheads are currently stationed in these three states, and may stay there under current agreements for the rest of the century. Before these weapons are ultimately removed to Russia, political upheaval in any or all of these states could provide an opening and a temptation for large-scale proliferation in all three. All nuclear weapons remaining in other successor states should be transferred to Russia as rapidly as possible, to be stored or dismantled according to the terms of START I and START II. The United States should help meet the costs of doing this job quickly and should also make it clear that a good result here will be essential for other kinds of help from the United States.

At home, an intensified program of reducing nuclear danger should be possible within a smaller over-all defense budget and a shift in financial priorities from nuclear to conventional forces. If the United States needs weapons that are more effective or more precise than the best conventional systems and the smallest tactical nuclear warheads in its current stockpile, it should seek them on the conventional side of the line. Finally, the United States should be a standard-setting financial con-tributor to a generally reinforced international system for the detection and frustration of such efforts to acquire nuclear weapons as those of Iraq and North Korea.

A fourth point is the need and opportunity for greatly increased openness on nuclear matters among all nations. There are indeed necessary secrets, but they are few, and they relate mainly to the protection of deployed systems—thus the location of a strategic submarine on patrol is a necessary and important secret. But the general atmosphere of secrecy that has surrounded the whole nuclear-weapon enterprise, in country after country, is unhealthy. It has had a destructive effect on the level of pub-lic understanding in every nuclear-weapon state, and it has also increased fear and mistrust between competing countries. Conversely, where there has been real improvement in nuclear relations, as between the United States and the former Soviet Union, a major element in the improvement has been a new openness, both inside each country and between the two. More broadly still, the history of the nuclear age, decade by decade, has shown that in free societies citizens can understand the changing realities of nuclear danger without any access to the few necessary secrets of any nuclear-weapon establishment. Such understanding, shared by citizens and their government, is much more valuable for our survival than most of our nuclear secrets. It is time for our government to take a conscious and active lead in such open discussion.

Fifth, the United States should join other nuclear-weapon states in giving up nuclear testing. We applaud President Bush's announcement in 1992 that there is no need for further U.S. nuclear tests to develop new weapon systems. We also support President Clinton's announcement of July 3, 1993, that the United States will not be the first to test, "at least through September of next year." The Clinton decision gives priority to an effort to negotiate a comprehensive test ban treaty that will weigh against proliferation, putting that goal ahead of the competing claim for safety testing, which we would otherwise support. We agree with this decision. The United States does not need new nuclear capabilities, and by supporting a nuclear test ban it strengthens its position among people whose help it needs to reduce nuclear danger.

Sixth, while we believe in close attention to the changing frontiers of science and technology, we do not believe in assuming that because a particular capability is desirable it must be attainable. We have made many constructive changes in our nuclear weapons systems since 1945, but we have also made excessive investments of money and hope in notions that were not well-grounded in scientific and technological reality. We address this topic more fully in chapter 3. The case we offer as a primary example of the way *not* to proceed is the Strategic Defense Initiative.

We end this overview with a warning based on our experience in working with problems of nuclear danger both in and out of government. The danger is massive and highly visible, and the objective, safety, is equally plain. The ways and means of reducing the danger are another matter altogether, and the decisions that matter most are those of governments, which are moved by many forces besides those of logic. The real world is complex, and what helps is only what can really happen.

Nonetheless, what is striking in this season is that there is now so much which meets that test. No one can say just what gains can be made when—and still less just how they will happen. One of the great lessons of the last few years is that change is sometimes fast and large and good—and also unexpected. What can be said now is that both hope and danger make this an extraordinarily good time for continued effort. That effort cannot be American alone, but it cannot be much without us.

Chapter 1

The Big Two—and Warheads in Successor States

T HE LARGEST AND MOST RADICALLY CHANGED NUCLEAR danger in the world today is the one inherited from the half-century in which the United States and the Soviet Union were the leaders of opposing camps in a vast cold war. The Cold War is over, but the bilateral nuclear inheritance remains. Between them the two sides still have some fifty thousand nuclear warheads, now about 95 percent of total world stock. A serious process of limitation and reduction has at last begun, but the roots of these deployments run deep. To understand both the opportunities and the difficulties of the present we must briefly review the history that has brought us where we are—*with* the enormous arsenals but *without* a nuclear war. We must understand first the intensity of the forty-year interconnection between nuclear competition and political cold war; second, the astonishing changes of the years after Mikhail Gorbachev came to power in 1985; and third, the new set of opportunities and dangers that have come with the political collapse of the Soviet Union and the emergence of Boris Yeltsin as the democratic leader of Russia.

THE BOMB AND THE COLD WAR

The atom bomb and the Cold War were both born at the end of World War II. Their simultaneous arrival was a historical coincidence; only by chance are the scientific advances that led to the discovery of fission in 1938 and the political forces that brought the United States and the Soviet Union into worldwide confrontation after the defeat of Hitler in the same decade or even the same century. But there it is: the American bomb was ready for use over Hiroshima in 1945, just as Soviet power was fastening itself on Eastern Europe behind what would soon be called the Iron Curtain. The Cold War and the bomb arrived together. In the 1990s, conversely, the end of the Cold War offers the largest opportunity yet for large-scale and lasting improvement in what has been the most dangerous, costly, and politically destructive of all the world's nuclear activities since the discovery of fission—the nuclear arms race between the United States and the Soviet Union. That improvement is currently well begun but quite unfinished, and not at all to be taken for granted.

In the interlocking history of the bomb and the Cold War, thinking about one always strongly affected thinking about the other. Now the end of the Cold War permits a great change in our view of the bomb. For both the United States and the Soviet Union, and for many countries, the Cold War was the defining political phenomenon of four decades. It was a general contest for power and influence in which the Soviet Union and the

United States became the primary opponents, each in alliance with a number of other countries. The Cold War never erupted into open warfare between the two primary opposing powers, but it was marked by almost every other kind of conflict and competition. There was warfare between allies of the two, in Korea and Vietnam, and U.S. forces were heavily engaged both times. There were bitter and sometimes bloody contests for political power in Europe, in Asia, and in what was loosely but revealingly called the Third World. There were crises over rights in Berlin and missiles in Cuba in which nuclear danger was intensely felt by sober leaders. In ways at once similar and different, each government encouraged its people's fear of the other. To an extent that is all the more apparent as it fades, the Cold War had a leading role in the domestic as well as the international lives of the two countries.

As a general and pervasive competition for power, the Cold War heavily affected the behavior of each superpower toward nuclear weapons. Given the assumption by each government that the other was deeply and even viciously hostile, it was natural that each should regard itself as gravely endangered by any nuclear armament of the other which was not promptly matched or outmatched by its own forces. Neither believed it could have trust for the other in such a life-and-death matter; each believed it must rely on itself. The initial effort at international control in 1946 was quickly destroyed by this absence of trust.

From this beginning the Cold War and the bomb reinforced each other in an interlocking process of fear and challenge which proved much stronger than successive efforts at arms control or detente. Each side insisted on attending to its nuclear security by its own means. That insistence led from the American A-bomb to the Soviet A-bomb in 1949, and then to a race for the H-bomb that both won technologically in the early 1950s. But neither won politically because neither could get decisively ahead. By the early 1960s both could make warheads more powerful—a thousand times Hiroshima—than military leaders found they really wanted. The competition shifted toward more sophisticated means of delivery: ballistic missiles (soon with multiple warheads), new basing modes like submarines, improved guidance and accuracy, and smaller warheads procured by the thousands for a wide range of military missions.

The two superpowers reached levels of survivable thermonuclear weaponry so high that nothing either of them could do could make a nuclear war between them anything but a shared catastrophe with no precedent in history; the forces arrayed by each made the choice of general nuclear war an act of national self-destruction. In each country influential groups continued to fear, from time to time, that "the other side" might get dangerously "ahead." Any technological initiative on one side could stir such fear on the other. But at least by 1975—presidents like Eisenhower, Kennedy, and Johnson would have said sooner—the strategic competition had in reality reached a durable stalemate, and in the following decade understanding of that reality was reinforced as successive alarms over various marginal changes proved overstated—examples include Soviet fear of American strategic defense and American fear of very large Soviet missiles.

Already in the 1950s the Americans had learned that in this competition the fundamental requirement for a national nuclear-weapon system is that it should be able to survive any attack and reply in force. During the Eisenhower administration this requirement for a survivable second-strike capability led to the development of forces survivable in three different and mutually reinforcing modes: bombers, missiles on land, and missiles in submarines. Each leg of this "triad" has been regularly modernized, and the level of reliance on this leg or that has changed from time to time, but there has been no real revolution in the perceived requirement for strategic deterrence since Eisenhower's time. The Soviet government, with a quite different balance of effort—its top preference was for land-based missiles—also deployed enormous and adequately survivable forces, and in the upshot each side has been amply deterred by the other. Survivable second-strike forces are still needed by both sides, but the size of those forces is now being reduced dramatically by negotiated agreement. No reduction yet considered by the two governments will disturb the continuing reality of strategic stalemate, and neither Russia nor the United States is likely to give up its requirement for survivable second-strike forces any time in the foreseeable future.

The stalemate imposed by the shared imperative of avoiding nuclear self-destruction was tested in the Cold War years not only by the continuing technological competition but also by repeated crises in which nuclear danger played a part. The most intense was the Cuban Missile Crisis of 1962, and its first lesson was that such a crisis should not be escalated. The second lesson was that the two sides should not pass this way again if they could avoid it. This double message was reinforced by the course and outcome of lesser crises earlier and later. A crisis might lead one side or the other to believe it needed more nuclear strength, as happened in Moscow after the Cuban crisis. But no crisis increased the desire of any later leader, on either side, to come close to nuclear war. The nuclear stalemate became clear *politically* as well as *technologically*.

Obstacles to Arms Control During the Cold War

Early efforts at U.S.–Soviet arms control met with only limited success. The limited test ban treaty of 1963 helped to protect the world's air from nuclear pollution but did not stop the continuing development of more sophisticated warheads by underground tests. The Antiballistic Missile Treaty of 1972 sharply limited defenses against strategic missiles. However, agreements constraining offensive weapons were temporary and of only limited effect, as each side protected its right to have the kinds of offensive capabilities that its military leaders valued most.

In the Cold War years political and nuclear competition reinforced each other. At the beginning Americans perceived the American bomb as an equalizer against the Red armies, but Stalin perceived it as a rude disturbance of the balance established by the victory of the same armies. The first Soviet explosion, in 1949, generated the American H-bomb, and the Soviet H-bomb went forward at the same time. A similar contest took place in bombers and in air defenses. The shock of the Soviet Sputnik in 1957 led to the American fear of a missile gap, a large American build-up in the early 1960s, and a large Soviet effort in the following years.

The nuclear competition also spread beyond "strategic" to "tactical" weapons of many kinds. Early decision-makers understandably believed that whenever a nuclear weapon could improve the chances of destroying a particular target, it should be at hand. This way of thinking had been used with every previous innovation in weaponry, from the slingshot to the musket to the machine gun to the heavy bomber. Pound for pound the nuclear warhead was at least ten thousand times more destructive than ordinary bombs or shells or missiles; why should not this destructiveness recommend it for all kinds of difficult missions?

The political stalemate that gradually became apparent in crisis behavior did not extend to the competition in development and deployment of nuclear warheads. Aircraft, submarines, missiles, and warheads were frequently modernized in strategic systems. At shorter ranges there was a continuing deployment of weapons with more limited missions. The United States came to have nuclear artillery shells, land-mines, depth charges, cruise missiles, and anti-aircraft weapons. A parallel evolution, different in detail, occurred on the Soviet side. What was missing, most of the time, was public attention to these less-than-strategic deployments. Choices about tactical warheads were usually made without much interference from political decision-makers who were not only heavily occupied by larger questions but also respectful of the intense commitment of each service to its own devices. There was a certain institutional prestige, in the early decades, in the possession of nuclear warheads, and no service wanted public debate about its own ways of having that prestige.

So it happened that for a long time too little attention was paid to the question of whether, and in what circumstances, a president would ever authorize the use of tactical weapons. Pushed aside was the reality that this question must be asked about every nuclear weapon of any kind, even those with apparently narrow missions. In that sense the primacy of political considerations was neglected in the process of military procurement.

A parallel and still broader impact of traditional military thinking was the persistence among military commanders and war-planners of the commitment to victory. They had not been trained to think of any kind of warfare as something to be avoided or "deterred" as intrinsically suicidal. They had been taught to fight to win. Those responsible for decisions about strategic deployment made plans and sought warheads and means of delivery that could be used, if necessary, to win. So did their Soviet adversaries. Partisans of strategic superiority were deeply resistant to the argument that no one could win an all-out nuclear war. They were planning to do exactly that. And even when it was clear to every one that a large-scale exchange of strategic warheads would cause tens of millions of casualties on both sides, the partisans of strategic superiority continued to argue that the "superior" side would gain decisive bargaining advantage from its ability to "prevail," in some sense, in any exchange.

We should not suppose that planners or commanders really wanted a large two-way exchange; they did what they could to have forces and plans that would limit the damage from the enemy, and their underlying hope was that adequate strength would prevent nuclear war by deterrence. Nonetheless, they did often think about the nuclear balance of power in conventional terms. Many argued that to be "ahead" in strategic capability would provide a decisive political advantage in time of crisis—in much the same way that the stronger fleet-in-being was thought politically decisive in the nineteenth century. The hope of advantage, together with the parallel fear of falling behind, worked powerfully to sustain a competition which in the end did no more than raise the cost of stalemate—a cost paid not only in dollars and rubles but also in the absorption of massive amounts of human energy and talent, and, more broadly, in the spread of fear and mutual mistrust.

Several points must be added in mitigation of this unpleasant history. First, no nuclear commander on either side ever failed to recognize and respect the ultimate authority of his head of state—the American president or the Soviet chairman. Second, no nuclear commander ever sought to increase the likelihood of nuclear war by deliberate provocation. Third, commanders on both sides, as the record demonstrates, were effectively attentive to the avoidance of warfare by accident (which is not to say that there were no moments of provocative error). Fourth, military commanders, as well as their civilian superiors, did gradually come to understand that general nuclear warfare would be a shared disaster on an unprecedented scale. Deep-seated awareness of this reality among senior commanders on both sides has been an important element in the constructive changes of the last decade.

The Nuclear Umbrella

For the United States, nuclear weapons had another Cold War role that went beyond the maintenance of strategic superiority or stalemate. Nuclear weapons were valued also as protection for allies with no such weapons of their own. The United States offered nuclear protection to non-nuclear friends in South Korea, in Japan, and above all in the North Atlantic alliance (NATO). These weapons were thought necessary not only to neutralize the Soviet nuclear threat but also to compensate for Soviet-bloc superiority in conventional strength. Above and beyond the notion of nuclear strength to deter *nuclear* attack, it became the doctrine of

NATO that only American readiness for nuclear response to *conventional* aggression could reliably deter the Soviet Union and its allies from some exercise of their heavy conventional superiority. Questions about theater nuclear forces for this additional kind of deterrence—often called "extended deterrence"—brought repeated debates within NATO and also a mutually disconcerting competition with the Soviet Union in nuclear-armed systems of theater range. Different administrations described this American policy differently, and there were varied American deployments. Recurrent alarms were sounded on both sides over changes in the capabilities of theater-range missiles.

In every administration there was a constantly asserted requirement that the United States must be ready to use nuclear weapons—first if necessary—in the defense of Europe. Throughout the Cold War, East-West confrontation had a nuclear edge in Europe. Occasionally the Soviet government sought to gain political advantage by deliberately arousing nuclear fear, and debates in the West sometimes had a similar if less intense effect. Among Europeans, arguments that comforted one listener could deeply disturb another. Those who feared the bomb more than the Red Army did not wish to hear of its possible use, while those who primarily feared Soviet strength were not comforted by any suggestion that the American bomb would not be available. In this way nuclear fears of different kinds became reciprocally reinforcing to each other in Cold War Europe.

EFFECTS OF SECRECY

A major element in this whole history was the intense secrecy surrounding nuclear weapons. The bomb had been conceived in secrecy, for the excellent reason that Hitler should not learn that the Americans thought it could be made and so be drawn toward making it himself. But the habit of secrecy took on a life of its own that persisted even after the basic secret had been made public with blinding force at Hiroshima on June 6, 1945. What warheads you had, and where, you did not say. You might do some boasting—especially, a particular branch of the armed forces might praise its own contribution—but you could and did claim secrecy when you wanted it. Others played the same game, especially in Moscow, where the general addiction to secrecy was already strong. Both sides became obsessed with keeping nuclear secrets from each other.

In the United States, both the government and the public too readily accepted the unfounded notion that "how to make a bomb" was an American secret that could somehow be kept. Starting with Harry Truman himself, Americans allowed themselves the presumptuous belief that the very existence of the bomb was a triumph of American know-how and not the inevitable result of a worldwide advance in the understanding of the physics and chemistry of fission.

There were indeed early American advantages, not only in ample resources and a location far from hostile aircraft but also in the understanding of particular technical complexities (there was also timely and crucial help from British and refugee scientists). In the early stages, intelligence on American research may well have saved some time for the Soviets. But the broader record now shows plainly that the Americans could keep no basic nuclear secrets for very long because they belonged to nature, not to their first finders, so that they were always open to discovery by first-class minds anywhere. Thus it was the mind of Andrei Sakharov and not Soviet espionage that was decisive in the rapid creation of the Soviet H-bomb.

But that is not what most Americans believed at the time. A misplaced belief in secrecy continued to feed a misplaced fear of espionage, and the war-born cult of concealment was destructively reinforced. It was not a healthy environment for the rational consideration of nuclear-weapons policy. In the later decades of the Cold War more sensible behavior developed, and the quality of public discussion improved, but there remained a considerable inheritance of unjustified belief that only experts with access to secrets could understand these matters.

CHANGES OF THE GORBACHEV ERA

The Gorbachev years—1985 to 1991—were extraordinary on many counts, and not least for the growing belief, as one change followed another, that what lay ahead might be still more startling than what had already happened. First and most important, there was a basic political movement within the Soviet Union, from the congealed and conformist party dictatorship of Brezhnev through the growing openness of *glasnost* to the emergence of a new politics of elections. Second, Moscow accepted the liberation of Eastern Europe, both from local communist domination and from Soviet military power. Third, there was an end of political cold war with the West, and in particular with the United States. Fourth, a policy of nuclear restraint emerged which led to agreements showing a new Soviet belief that steady reduction in the number of nuclear weapons on both sides was greatly in the interest of the Soviet Union.

Taken together, and combined with a responsive set of American steps, these changes produced dramatic reductions in the level and intensity of nuclear danger between the two superpowers. From 1985 onward, Reagan and Gorbachev together took the lead in seeking a new relationship between the two governments. The Intermediate Nuclear Forces (INF) Treaty of 1987 eliminated a whole new class of missiles that could be delivered in each direction across Europe. In 1990 the many parties to the Cold War in Europe joined in a treaty limiting conventional forces in Europe (CFE Treaty), thus giving formal international endorsement to the end of the Warsaw Pact's perceived conventional superiority, which had led NATO to fearful reliance on nuclear deterrence. In 1991 a large-scale, bilateral, strategic arms reduction of some 30 percent was also negotiated and agreed upon, in START I—a comprehensive treaty of unprecedented scope, with arrangements for verification even more remarkable than the reductions themselves. Because of these and other changes in Soviet behavior, it seemed reasonable by the summer of 1991 to believe that there was genuine and solid conviction behind Gorbachev's acceptance and affirmation of the phrase Ronald Reagan had repeated at every opportunity since 1982: "A nuclear war cannot be won and must never be fought." Much remained unfinished and uncertain, but the overall movement away from untrusting competitive stalemate was clear. The events in the six years after Gorbachev came to power seemed to be a high-speed reversal of the long, slow process that had built and sustained the Cold War strategic competition.

In the last five months of 1991 the pace of historic change accelerated still further. In the middle of August, old-time communists in the USSR attempted a counterrevolution. Within three days their attempt had failed. The communist party collapsed, and in the aftermath it soon became clear that decisive power had shifted from the old Soviet center—from Gorbachev—to the leaders of the constituent states of the Union. By the end of the year the Soviet Union had ceased to exist. There were fifteen successor states, of which eleven, including Russia, joined in a new Commonwealth of Independent States (CIS), but that Commonwealth soon proved to have little central power.

These enormous changes ended the threat presented in the Cold War by the conventional superiority of the Soviet bloc, and so ended the urgently felt need for American deterrence of that threat by a readiness to use nuclear weapons. The possibility of a Soviet-bloc war against NATO and the stated requirement for the United States to be willing to initiate nuclear warfare were overtaken by the massive change in the balance of European power and the massive reduction in Russian-American hostility. With U.S. nuclear strength now needed only to balance the nuclear strength of others, the United States was free to pursue the reduction and limitation of all nuclear arsenals including its own. No one could say that the Russian threat to Europe would never reappear, but no one could say it was immediate, and the nuclear result was clear: Americans could accept balanced nuclear reductions without fear for European security, as long as they could be sure of having ample warning of any reversal of the great events of 1989–1991. The clear *political* interest of the United States was to help the newly peaceable and democratic Russia to survive and gain in stability.

The United States quickly came to have two nuclear policies toward the former Soviet Union. One was aimed at progress in major reductions agreed with Russia, the principal inheritor of Soviet power and the state that contained most but not all of the nuclear weapons and installations. The other policy was aimed at encouraging and assisting a safe and timely end of the deployment of nuclear weapons outside Russia. Some of the more important American steps reflected both aims, but it will be useful here to treat the two questions separately. In nuclear affairs it makes a great difference whether the other party to any relationship sees itself as a nuclear-weapon state. Russia is and will remain a nuclear-weapon state, but the other newly independent states, the United States believed, could be encouraged to make a different choice.

THE NEW RUSSIAN-AMERICAN BALANCE

In the eighteen months after the signing of START I in July 1991, the United States and Russia reached two new understandings of unprecedented range. The first was a "Joint Understanding" of June 1992 which led to the START II Treaty in January 1993; START II prescribed a major further reduction of strategic weapons. The second, less formal and more innovative, was a pair of announcements, a few days apart in the fall of 1991, of sweeping American and Soviet reductions of tactical nuclear weapons. Both signalled large changes in basic nuclear policy on both sides.

We begin with the more familiar matter of strategic reductions. We have already noted the signing of START I. That treaty was the product of nine years of negotiation, the first and probably the last treaty of its kind. It has 250 pages of text, annexes, and protocols—all part of the treaty—and it is buttressed by another thirty pages of related agreements, letters, correspondence, joint statements, other statements, and declarations. It provides for a reduction of about one-third in the strategic warheads of both the Soviet Union and the United States, to a total on each side of 6,100 to 8,600 warheads. The formal treaty limit is 6,000, but there are counting rules that allow more warheads when they are carried in "slow flyers" like bombers—thus an airplane with only "ordinary" nuclear bombs counts as one warhead, no matter how many it actually has on board.

There are many novel constraints in the START I treaty, aimed at reducing forces or capabilities particularly feared by one side or the other. The most notable for Americans is a 50 percent reduction in the warheads carried by Soviet heavy intercontinental ballistic missiles (ICBMs)—the SS-18s. The treaty is also remarkable for its comprehensive provisions on verification, including data exchanges and on-site inspection.

It was generally believed at the time that START I would not be followed by further reductions at any early date, but in the first six months of 1992, the leaders of the United States and Russia laid the foundation for a second strategic agreement that moved far beyond START I. Beginning with new proposals by President Bush in January, the negotiations led on, with major contributions from both sides, to an agreement in principle reached between Presidents Bush and Yeltsin in Washington on June 16, 1992.

After a lull during the American election season, negotiations were renewed at the end of 1992, and the START II treaty was signed in early January 1993. Under START II each side will reduce its strategic warheads to a number of its own choice between 3,000 and 3,500, and both sides will eliminate land-based missiles with multiple warheads. The low limits were desired primarily by the Russians, and the elimination of multiple-warhead ICBMs—especially the remaining SS-18s—was what the Americans wanted most. One does not know whether to be more astonished by the speed or the sweep of this achievement.

It is likely that START II will be the last major agreement for some time in this process of bilateral strategic reductions. The reductions required by the new agreements are scheduled to take seven to ten years. Learning to cooperate in all the new ways required— sharing of information, executing "exhibitions" and "inspections," avoiding or resolving disagreements— will also take time.

The limits of START II—3,000 to 3,500 war-heads—are not the lowest that can be achieved between the United States and Russia. In chapter 3 we argue that both sides could have confidence in the stability and sufficiency of significantly lower limits. The present priority, however, should be the orderly and mutually confident execution of all the reductions required under START I and II. Obviously the current schedules are not sacred, and it may turn out that both sides can gain from moving more rapidly. Nonetheless the direction of change—toward reductions, confidence, and openness—is more important in this bilateral undertaking than speed.

The two sides must also learn to live with the arrangement on tactical nuclear weapons that was worked out in the early fall of 1991, not by formal agreement, but by an exchange of broadcast speeches by President Bush on September 27 and President Gorbachev on October 5. Both spoke in ways that recognized the growing role of Boris Yeltsin as president of Russia.

President Bush announced the most far-reaching set of one-sided reductions and restraints in the nuclear age. Among them were the withdrawal and destruction of all land-based tactical warheads and all naval nuclear depth charges, the withdrawal and storage of all other naval nuclear warheads for cruise missiles or aircraft, and the removal from alert status of all strategic bombers and all the ballistic missiles slated for removal under START I. Under these unilateral decisions, over 3,000 U.S. weapons will be destroyed, 950 stored, and 2,690 taken off alert. Eight days later Gorbachev announced a broadly parallel set of destructions, reductions and removals from alert status, with such added proposals of his own as a one-year moratorium on nuclear testing. Taken together these two unilateral announcements were the largest changes ever made in less-than-strategic forces. They were notable not only as the first major effort at arms control by separate unilateral announcements but also, more substantively, because they promised a large-scale reduction in deployments of warheads that presented special problems in command and control and, in some cases, safety.

Reinforcing the Bush-Gorbachev proposals was the support of the American initiative by the Joint Chiefs of Staff and the apparent parallel approval of Russian military leaders. Absent the Cold War—absent a rival competing with all arms everywhere—military men appeared content to take tactical nuclear warheads off the board (with the probably temporary exception of American tactical aircraft in Europe). For the Americans the experience of the Gulf War was surely relevant; they had learned in the Gulf what their best conventional forces could do, and it was more than enough. In a relationship without the mistrust and hostility of the Cold War, the U.S. Navy would be better off in all the seas and oceans without tactical warheads to attend to on board, and free of the fear of Soviet forces with such warheads.

For a long time there had been advocates of arms control by reciprocal unilateral steps. Here the two leaders took that road in a set of actions much larger than was expected by any one outside the circle of decision. Nothing could show more clearly how much change there was in the basic nuclear relationship of the United States and the Soviet Union. The fear of dangerous unilateral concession, so strong in the Cold War years, was replaced by a shared recognition that these tactical deployments were both unnecessary and potentially dangerous. More broadly the Bush initiative revealed a new, post–Cold War standard for the assessment of the less-than-strategic nuclear weapons systems that the United States does and does not need. It does not need tactical weapons, this decision shows, that give instant on-the-spot readiness to fight a nuclear war anywhere its forces find themselves.

Only one basic requirement remains for the strategic forces of the superpowers: they should be considered fully adequate, in each country, to ensure against strategic attack from the other. This deterrent requirement has been central for both sides throughout the nuclear age, and today it is the only one left that matters. Neither side now asks that its strategic forces be able it to win some general nuclear war, because both sides now recognize openly that in such a war there would be only losers. The lesser capabilities that either side may require of its nuclear weapons—for example, deterrence of some lesser nuclear threat by some other possessor of nuclear weapons—do not affect the overall size of their strategic forces. An American force that is sufficient to balance the Russian force, until both sides make reductions far beyond those now in sight, will be capable enough for every lesser job.

The same thing is now true on the Russian side. During the Cold War it was possible to think that Soviet planners must consider the nightmare of having to face three or four strategic nuclear enemies at the same time. They certainly had deep political differences with all four of the other announced nuclear-weapon states—the United States, Britain, France, and China. But there is no justification for such Russian nightmares today.

Despite the great reductions now in prospect, there is no early prospect of escape from the need to maintain a superpower balance—albeit at much lower levels. A great deal of work remains to be done in reaching the lower levels of deployment now projected, and it is important not to be misled by unachievable objectives. Fifty years of experience argue strongly against any confidence in extreme solutions. In particular there is no early escape through either the achievement of strategic superiority or the abolition of nuclear weapons. This proposition is important because all through the nuclear age each objective has had its passionate supporters, and because very often the terms of public discussion have been framed by the contest between these two sides.

Of these two realities, the one that is at once easier to understand and harder to accept is that there is no present hope of proceeding quickly to a world without nuclear weapons. Even if Russia and the United States were the only two nuclear powers and had only each other to consider, they could not now aim for the complete elimination of their nuclear arsenals. Which side would believe that it could trust the other not to have hidden one, or ten, or a hundred warheads? If one side did cheat in this fashion and the other did not, would not the cheater have a decisive advantage if there should be renewed hostility between the two? Until levels of trust and openness across national boundaries are much higher than they are today, this inescapable possibility truly and thoroughly blocks any zero-zero solution to the problem of nuclear balance. In today's real world of six to eight nuclear-weapon states, the zero-zero solution is still more unmanageable. Moreover, the lower limit imposed by imperfect trust is well above zero. Each government will always want a level of nuclear strength such that no sudden secret effort by "the other side" to break out could in fact create a decisive change in the balance of power.

Although getting to zero has always had its true believers, simply because the continuing nuclear competition seems so dangerous and unrewarding, this objective has not had the same influence as the belief that nuclear warheads are such a decisive form of military power that the right policy is to get and keep a meaningful superiority. Such superiority is exactly what many Americans thought they had after the bomb's existence was revealed at Hiroshima. It is not now a reasonable objective for any country.

Both the United States and Russia must accept the reality that both countries will have strategic nuclear forces for many years ahead. Leaders on both sides must still think of each other's weapons as a potential future threat, and they must also take account of the weapons of Britain, France, China, and the smaller nuclear powers. Political leaders, especially in Russia, must also think of what their military commanders will say and do. A time of trouble that includes danger from the right is not a likely time for Russian political leaders to attempt to impose unlimited unilateral nuclear disarmament.

How, then, should we begin to think about the question of long-run Russian and American forces? It is clear on both sides that needs are now different, and less, but it is another matter for each to decide just what forces it still does need. Almost from the beginning, nuclear forces have been sized and shaped in each country in relation to those of the other side. Of course there have been many other elements in procurement decisions—the interests of a particular service, the emergence of new technical possibilities, the natural tendency of designers and commanders to want weapons that are faster, more destructive, or more accurate—but in a larger sense the imperative requirement has always been not to fall behind.

In the new world after the Cold War, it is still right to say that the United States must not fall behind Russia. The U.S. government must ensure that Russia never has reason to think it has a nuclear advantage that could be used against the United States if some enormous change in Moscow should produce renewed hostility between the two countries. Even with all its other problems, Russia will want to have the same confidence about its nuclear relation to the United States. Each country must feel safe against renewed nuclear fear of the other.

This requirement is met today, on both sides, by the forces in being, and also by the forces that will remain in being after the START treaties take effect. In the American case, the standards of performance required of U.S. strategic forces do not impose any requirement for early large-scale replacement of any part of the strategic nuclear force by a new delivery system—not a new airplane beyond those on order, not a new submarine beyond those already under construction, and not a new land-based missile. Only the prospective deployment of large-scale Russian offensive or defensive forces with a wholly new set of capabilities could change this situation any time soon; there is no such prospect today, and we should have ample warning if it began to develop. The Russian forces will remain similarly adequate. It is clear that both sides can help themselves and each other by moving down to the newly agreed levels. The two governments have not yet explained much about their reasons for the 3,000 to 3,500 level, but others have advocated similar levels with substantial supporting analysis.

What is important here, perhaps more important than numbers of warheads or exact divisions of strength between one leg of the triad and another, is that present requirements for a strategic nuclear deterrent are not the same as those that have seemed important to decision-makers in earlier decades. What each side requires is a force so constituted that a wholly sufficient number of warheads could always survive and strike back. Neither side need seek to win, because winning is understood to be impossible. Top-level control over any use of nuclear weapons will remain enormously important as long as such weapons exist. Command-and-control should be improved as technology permits, so that it can be more varied and less vulnerable than what exists today. But there is no need for a steady series of new systems of delivery, each more expensive than the one before. The START treaties lay a base for shared strategic moderation, for a stable and peaceable balance, at a great long-run reduction in cost, tension, and danger.

As we move toward this new balance, each side will be tempted to revert to the competitive habits of thought that developed so strongly in the years in which this or that marginal advantage seemed worth defending, not only against the other side but sometimes still more intensely against those who seemed soft in one's own government. Such habits can obstruct the ways of thinking that are now appropriate.

Consider the American domestic debate. After decades of verbal and political combat between ardent believers in arms control and ardent supporters of expanded and steadily modernized systems for both delivery and defense, many on each side have learned to see the other side as the enemy. This result is natural. On the one hand those responsible for ensuring that the military—in particular their own branch of the military—plays its full role in strategic deterrence have naturally been advocates of large deployments, regularly modernized and armed with the best available warheads. A few are still reluctant to abandon war-fighting doctrines, and some are still advocates of strategic defense. Conversely, those who regard the bomb itself as the enemy still tend to favor further limitations whenever it is politically possible, and sometimes when it is not. In the years of intense—and intensely debated—nuclear competition, there developed habits of sustained intellectual conflict which are now badly out of date. This war is now ripe for settlement because the new situation permits so much common ground. The widespread support of START II among experts who have often been divided in the past argues that there can now be large changes supported by both sides.

An even more striking sign of progress may be the decision of the Bush administration in the summer of 1992 to announce that there is no need for further underground testing to develop new warheads. This decision was followed by congressional action that sharply limits future testing, primarily to the improvement of safety, and opens the prospect of reaching an early comprehensive test ban treaty. Such legislation would have been hotly contested, and probably rejected by Congress, only a few years ago. In 1992 it found solid support.

The debates on the Russian side are not reported as well as our own, but it is clear that not every Russian commander was enthusiastic about such a dramatic change as the elimination of the large SS-18 missile. The SS-18 is the most notable example of a weapon that was destabilizing in its basic design because it was at once enormously destructive and inescapably vulnerable. Carrying many warheads with high yields, it was a lucrative target; its fixed base made it an *easy* target. Two opposing forces of this sort would be inherently unstable because the side that fired first might indeed achieve an instant and crushing superiority. This never became possible, because neither side relied only on such weapons and because congressional opposition sharply limited the deployment of the American "answer" to the SS-18, the ten-warhead MX missile. Nonetheless the multi-warhead, silo-based missile was an excellent target for arms control.

The true interest of both sides is that each step toward lower and less threatening deployments should be seen as a step forward by healthy majorities on both sides, so that nuclear moderation remains for both, as it was in 1992, a broadly popular policy. In particular the United States should avoid the temptation to use a time of great Russian economic stress to drive for one-sided advantages, either by negotiation or appropriation. The years immediately ahead would be a particularly bad time for Americans, whether by unilateral action or unbalanced agreements or both, to make the mistake of "piling on." At any levels now in prospect any marginal advantages so obtained would have no real value, and their political damage could be serious. Complaints against such "advantages" supposedly gained by the other side have helped hard-liners to gain strength in both countries in the past. A time of general political success is not a time to risk that success by bargaining overreach. The execution of the new agreements will be a good time for care, fairness, and openness on both sides, but especially on the side that is *not* internally threatened by reactionary counterrevolution.

The simplest guideline for Americans may be that we should explicitly determine that our own strategic nuclear deployment need never be greater than that of the Russians. The maintenance of equality is wholly defensible, and it is politically familiar. It is not likely to fuel political resentment on either side. The economic and military priorities now working for nuclear moderation may well be stronger in Russia than in the United States, but it will be to the general American advantage, throughout the process of reduction, to be ready to go as far as the Russians. The importance of other familiar criteria may go up as numbers of warheads come down: survivability, safety, absence of hair-trigger danger and others; these are well protected in START I and II.

The largest threat to the success of this ongoing undertaking is that there could come a time when strong resistance or resentment, on one side or the other, could lead to a breakdown of the cooperative reduction of forces and a renewal of the fearful interlocking competition that marked the nuclear arms race. If that should happen, the Cold War itself would also be renewed.

On the evidence thus far, however, the policy of large-scale reduction has broad support in both countries. Both want nuclear deployments that are less dangerous, less expensive, and smaller. Both have better things to do with scarce resources, and specifically more urgent military needs. Both are now competing downward, not upward, and that sort of competition is relatively easy to conduct. The START II negotiation itself shows a good way to deal with such competition. The Americans initially proposed a limit of 4,700 warheads, and the Russians proposed 2,500; the final agreement says that each country will go down to a number between 3,000 and 3,500. If Russia does go down to 3,000, it would be sensible for the Americans also to get down to that level. The truth is that when the strategic balance is stable, the side that keeps the somewhat smaller force is the smart one; it saves money without risk.

Even in such a cooperative process there is plenty of room for misunderstanding and a resulting need for close attention by senior members of both governments. Both sides now praise openness, but both have much to learn about its practice. Both sides have learned from experience that it helps to be straight with one another, but the whole history of Russian-American relations shows us that not every politician or diplomat or military leader understands the importance of such straightness. It is certain that in the reduction process there will be points of difference and disagreement; both sides must be ready for them, and disagreements must be pulled up to a level where the decision-makers on each side understand the common interest in getting things straightened out.

A particularly sensitive area that will need watching is that of less-than-strategic forces, where formal agreements do not exist, but where the two sides made unilateral announcements in 1991 that clearly depend in some degree upon each other. There may be arguments in each government for modification of these announced plans, sometimes for reasons not involving any desire to get ahead of the other side. These unilateral undertakings are not formally binding, but departing from them will damage bilateral understanding unless there are careful arrangements for explanation and a readiness to accept parallel changes on the other side. What is crucial is that any changes should be announced and explained.

Openness of this kind is not an easy or altogether natural process in international behavior, and it is important to use this time of relatively easy reductions for learning by experience. Fortunately recent years offer much evidence that this course of action now has the support of public opinion in both countries. Moreover the nearer you get to the top in both governments, the more likely you are to find understanding of the depth and breadth of the interest that both countries have in strengthening their new cooperation in nuclear restraint.

The process of working together in this new way is much more urgent business than new negotiations on reductions beyond those now in prospect. In the short run there is plenty to do in executing safely and securely what is now the program of both sides, and a great deal to be learned in the process. Political energy and courage will be needed to deal with unexpected but probable difficulties and misunderstandings. Further American financial assistance will be needed, like the $400 million a year that was voted in the Defense appropriation in 1991 and again in 1992, on the initiative of Senators Nunn (D.-Georgia) and Lugar (R.-Indiana), for help in dismantling Soviet nuclear systems. Both governments will gain from treating this whole enterprise as a shared undertaking in the reduction of nuclear danger. They will be reinforced in this basic approach if they bear in mind that the visible and sustained practice of their own bilateral arms reduction, openness, and political cooper-

ation is indispensable to their effective participation as
leaders—though never the only leaders—in the broader
international effort against nuclear danger.

PROTECTION AGAINST RELAPSE

The new U.S.-Russian nuclear relationship must meet
one further and quite different requirement: it must
leave each side clearly able to protect itself against the
risk that the other might renew the intense nuclear competition of the Cold War. As we have suggested, the
nuclear relationship now developing—so much of it
already "post–Cold War" in nature—is itself a powerful
safeguard against such relapse, as are the recent political
changes both inside the former Soviet Union and in Eastern Europe. Nonetheless a conservative counterrevolution in Russia is possible, and it could lead both to
political hostility and to a renewal of nuclear competition. American confidence in the present course of sustained
and shared reductions requires American confidence
that there would be plenty of time for appropriate
responses to any such reversal of current hopes.

In nuclear matters the basic protection against any
renewed arms race lies in the reality that for as far ahead
as we are now able to see, the United States, along with Russia, will retain a strategic nuclear deterrent such that neither side could hope to achieve any significant nuclear
advantage without giving obvious notice of its effort
early enough to give plenty of time for a balancing reply.
That is true today, and it will also be true under START I
and II. If negotiations are even moderately prudent, it
will be true also under any later and more modest regime
including other nuclear powers. The best evidence of this
reality is the record of superpower competition during

the height of the Cold War. There was never any deployment on either side that was not promptly detected on the other, and although there were frequent political alarms in each country over the danger in the opponent's deployments, there was in fact not a single case on either side where a change in the strategic balance had any substantial political or military effect on the course of the Cold War. The most that any build-up did was to stimulate both fear and response on the other side. The strategic stalemate remained intact. Both sides, in the future that is opening, can keep sustained assurance that there will be no nuclear break-out on either side without warnings that give more than enough time for any necessary response. There are indeed special cases where the need for such assurance must override traditional habits of secrecy. An example is the need for assurance that downloaded multiple-warhead missiles are not secretly uploaded, but the example makes our point; this kind of reassurance can be achieved if both sides give it the priority it deserves, and the case of downloading is specifically covered in START I and II by special monitoring provisions.

Get Rid of Fast-Flyers?

In the long run, the United States and Russia can go still further in the reduction of the nuclear danger between them, although the measures that will help most in the long run may not be the same as those that make urgent sense today. An excellent example of this possible difference is the long-range ballistic missile, the "fast-flyer" that can cross the world in half an hour. In the agreements of 1991 and 1992, neither side was willing to give up long-range missiles entirely for the excellent reason that for both of them such missiles are currently the most survivable single system of delivery. Survivability is properly prized as an essential element in strategic stability; technically what keeps each side safely deterred is that the other side can always reply. Both sides have agreed that the multi-warhead, silo-based missile is unstable; it is a dangerously vulnerable target; two warheads, in principle, could make a successful attack on ten. But long-range missiles that are survivable, such as those on submarines at sea or on mobile systems on land, are still greatly prized and relied on by each side. Thus the United States is preserving more warheads on Trident missiles at sea than anywhere else, and the Russian preference for long-range missiles may be even stronger.

This current preference is reasonable because strategic survivability is crucial to both sides and currently obtainable in no other way, but over time it will make good sense to examine the ways and means of getting away from this dependence on fast-flyers. As long as they are with us, neither side can escape the possibility of a sudden surprise attack in which unrecallable warheads arrive thirty minutes after launching. In spite of careful technology and the sanity and sobriety of those in control of such forces, this possibility will exist as long as the weapons exist, and it will shadow both the peace of the two nations and the peace of mind of their citizens. The intrinsic danger of long-range fast-flyers becomes even more apparent if we consider what could happen if they should become available, along with nuclear warheads, to some future Saddam Hussein.

Personal discomfort with fast-flyers led Reagan and Gorbachev at Reykjavik in 1986 to a brief but intense exploration of their complete elimination. Their discussions foundered on their differences over strategic defense. There was also no systematic attack on the problem of ensuring the survivability of deterrent forces using other means of delivery. Nonetheless the Reykjavik discussion was farsighted if incomplete, and one of the advantages of the current process of mutually supportive reduction is that both sides can consider again the long-run advantage of a world without long-range fast-flyers. The reductions in START II will themselves greatly reduce the number of fast-flyers, and neither side can ignore the fact that if and when the number of fast-flyers gets to *zero,* the survivability of long-range aircraft goes way up because the worst threat to the bomber base is the ballistic missile. There are complexities in this analysis, and reasons for proceeding with care, but if survivability can otherwise be assured, the complete removal of long-range fast-flyers would ease both the danger and the mental strain of life with thermonuclear weapons.

Long-range missiles are of course not deployed only by Russia and the United States. There are missiles in other countries that have nuclear warheads to put on them. The renunciation of long-range ballistic missiles would have to be worldwide, but fortunately the development and testing of such large missiles can be effectively monitored. There will not, however, be much international progress away from long-range missiles while Washington and Moscow continue to rely on them.

Is It Safe to Reduce Bilateral Nuclear Danger?

It is generally assumed that for the American public reducing nuclear danger is a good purpose in itself, and also good for its effect in strengthening the newly friendly relations between Russia and the United States. But there are many who have believed that nuclear danger has not been all bad through the Cold War years. Did not nuclear danger make one side or the other more cautious in this or that crisis?

There are arguments on this question, but there are not many close students of the Cold War or direct participants in its larger crises who would deny that in moments of confrontation the existence of the nuclear possibility helped to make the leaders on both sides more careful. Both sides have had an evidently different purpose in recent years: the reduction of cost and danger by reducing the two enormous forces and improving their stability and survivability. Will these changes, and still more the ones we suggest for the future, reduce the peace-keeping impact of those same forces?

There are really two questions here, one about the past and one about the future. The honest answer to the question about the past is that nuclear danger did have some constraining impact on Cold War crises. But insofar as that impact came from fear of some unpredictable detonating event in the continuing Cold War context, we are all better off without it. And insofar as it was a more sober awareness of what could happen if the two powers ever began armed warfare with one another, it will continue to exist, even at much more modest levels of nuclear strength.

The decisive point is that lower and more stable forces are preferable not only for themselves but for their contribution to keeping the Cold War from revival and avoiding any recurrence of past confrontations such as those over Berlin and Cuba. If we do slide back to cold war, then indeed we will slide back into life with a renewed sense of nuclear danger and nuclear competition between the United States and Russia. But now we are headed in a more hopeful direction, and the object of policy should be to stay on that course, in company with our new friends in Russia. The absence of the Cold War is a better guarantee of peace than the presence of imminent nuclear danger.

RUSSIAN NUCLEAR STRENGTH
AS A POST–COLD WAR STABILIZER

One major peace-keeping element in post–Cold War
Europe which students of nuclear danger should observe
with respect is the role of Russian nuclear weapons as a
defense of Russia itself, at a time when the Russian government might otherwise feel gravely threatened by
changes in the nearby world. Before the nuclear age
changes like those that occurred in Eastern Europe
between 1989 and 1992 would have been regarded as so
threatening to Russian power and position that they
almost surely would have led to war. That would have been
the expectation and the confident prediction of realist
scholars and statesmen familiar with the world of the
European powers in the prenuclear centuries. But it did not
happen—or even come close to happening—that way.
There are many reasons for Russian restraint in these
years of enormous change: the lack of any will-to-war
among the newly awakened citizens of Russia is a most
important one, closely connected to the intensely
remembered experience of World War II. Also notable,
however, is Moscow's understanding that the changes in
Eastern Europe, enormous as they were, could not
become a direct threat to Russia because the Russian
bomb would still be on guard. Americans accustomed to
thinking of the Soviet bomb as a threat to others should
remind themselves that it has an entirely different and
much more comforting meaning to the government of
Russia, a country that, unlike our own, has vivid
national memories of the suffering inflicted by opponents exercising their conventional superiority at Russian
expense on Russian land. Russia's bomb well and truly pro-
tects her from any such threat, though it is important to

note that this mission can be discharged just as well with a force of three thousand warheads as with one of thirty thousand. The Russian case may be the most important of its kind, but chapter 2 shows that the defensive and peacekeeping bomb can be found in other countries too.

Ensuring Responsible Command and Control in Russia

In most discussions of nuclear danger it is taken for granted that nuclear-weapon states, in their own interest, will maintain tight and effective control over all nuclear weapons systems, so that there will be no unauthorized nuclear explosion. It seems clear that this kind of control is now exercised in both Russia and the United States, and both governments are entitled to be pleased by their cooperation in ensuring that the tactical weapons of the former Soviet Union have all been moved to Russia. The question that now arises is whether and how far the security of Russian warheads can be protected against the dangers inherent in the possibilities of revolt, anarchy, and counterrevolution in Russia itself. The likelihood of these internal political possibilities is uncertain, but even a small probability of disrupted or usurped control, when it relates to nuclear warheads and delivery systems, is important enough to deserve careful attention. What can be done about it?

The full answer here extends beyond the immediate nuclear field. Every country that might be endangered by a breakdown of responsible authority in Russia—and obviously the United States is such a country—has a strong interest in the survival and success of a moderate Russian government in clear command of a loyal and responsible military organization able to ensure the effective control of nuclear weapons that has marked both Soviet and Russian performance so far. This basic political objective is certainly supported by a process of arms control that continues to show respect for the reality of Russian nuclear strength. There is much to be gained by expanding and deepening the professional military connections between Russians and Americans that have developed in recent years. There is also much value, in this context, in reducing or even eliminating forces on alert on both sides. But neither good military relations nor a non-alert posture will necessarily continue if wild men come to power in Russia or take control of even a few nuclear weapons. The prevention of such an occurrence is in the first instance the responsibility and the deep national interest of the Russians themselves. What the United States can do about this danger depends mainly on what our friends in the present Moscow government want us to do. Russia will need much more American help before its democratic future is assured—help that includes, but is not limited to, all appropriate nuclear cooperation. The end of the Cold War and the reduction of nuclear danger that followed were made possible by the collapse of communism and the rise of much more democratic government. To keep nuclear danger down in Russia, the United States must do its full part to help to ensure that Russian democracy survives and grows strong. The design of the right kind of American help to Russia is a task beyond the scope of this book, but it is help that is fully justified by the question of the Russian nuclear future all by itself.

THE OTHER NEWLY INDEPENDENT STATES OF THE FORMER SOVIET UNION

The United States, Russia, and the three other successor states of the Soviet Union with nuclear warheads still on their territory—Ukraine, Belarus, and Kazakhstan—are formally agreed that the latter should be non-nuclear states, leaving Russia as the one nuclear-weapon state to succeed the Soviet Union. All the tactical nuclear weapons in these three and other successor states are officially reported to have been quickly moved to Russia. The three states besides Russia in which strategic weapons are still based have all agreed that they will accede to the Non-Proliferation Treaty as non-nuclear-weapon states and that all strategic weapons should be removed to Russia according to an agreed timetable. On the surface, this is excellent progress, but there are still reasons for concern. Thousands of strategic warheads remain in these three states and may stay there, under the rules agreed so far, for the rest of the century. In the interim there could be disconcerting political changes in any of these states, and any remaining weapons will continue by their very existence to suggest to these governments that there may be some advantage to be gained by delaying their departure, or even taking them over.

There is no previous case of such a situation. In all other countries the temptation to go nuclear has always had to compete with the reality that developing the weapons takes time, costs much money, and can stimulate un-wanted competition. In these cases the weapons already exist inside each state, though they remain under central command from Moscow, and it is only too easy to frame arguments that might be offered by those in the three states who would like to take over some or all of them:

1. They are as much ours as Russia's—we too are a successor to the old Soviet Union.

2. They will give us protection against Russia, and standing among all nations.

3. This decision is ours to make, like the parallel decisions of all earlier nuclear-weapon states.

There are strong countervailing arguments, of course, but such challenges are already being made to the existing commitments of the present governments. Until the danger is ended by the removal of the weapons, the possibility of large-scale proliferation will exist in all three states.

The nuclear systems that are the source of danger and temptation in these states should be transferred to Russia as rapidly as possible, to be stored or dismantled under the terms of existing or amended agreements between Russia and the United States. The United States should deepen its commitment to help meet the incremental costs of doing this job quickly, and it should also make sure the decision-makers in these states understand that rapid action will promote, while delay will retard or even prevent, other kinds of American support. This is not a matter merely of policy preferences in any one administration; it is a matter of what the American people will now permit in relations with future nuclear proliferators. The principle here is exactly the same as the one already set forth in the broader context of U.S.-Russian relations: our larger interest in political and economic progress is inseparably connected to our particular interest in reducing nuclear danger; working for each supports work for the other, and the two goals are not likely to be reached separately.

A policy of this sort will not be easy to execute, but it will be easier now than later. In 1992 the principle that Ukraine, Belarus, and Kazakhstan would be non-nuclear was formally and repeatedly affirmed by all three states. Since that is agreed, there can hardly be any objection in principle to the argument that the safe and sane way to reach this objective is to do it promptly, and with American help. The danger which urges speed here is a danger intrinsic to the uncertainties in the political future of these new states; recognizing this danger does not imply any challenge to the good faith of the acceptance of non-nuclear status by the present governments. Nor will rapid action damage any real interest of the three states; in the end they would find nothing but new expense and danger in becoming nuclear-weapon states. All their neighbors would be alarmed; their own peoples would be harshly divided; they would face unprecedented difficulties and dangers in handling the weapons they took over. Nor would these weapons in fact protect them from what they may fear most—the hostility of Russia. Their possession of nuclear weapons would only ensure that hostility and create a barrier of mutual suspicion that would prevent the good relations with Russia that all these states need.

These basic realities make it a deep common interest of all concerned—Russia, the United States, and the three republics—that all warheads in the three republics should revert to Russia as quickly as possible. All concerned should help in that process, as in the subsequent process of nuclear clean-up throughout the former Soviet Union. The temptation of nuclear status is understandable, but fraudulent. It is no disservice to the citizens of these three states that the American government should weigh in continuously and energetically on the side of the rapid removal of all the strategic warheads now on their lands.

IN SUMMARY: SUSTAINED COOPERATION FOR CONTROLLED MODERATION

The new nuclear relationships described and advocated here are strange—unfamiliar even to the governments that have been learning to work together in these new ways. Nonetheless, they are sound and promising because they rest on a deeply shared interest: that there should now be stability and confidence regarding nuclear weapons for all who shared in the very different past of the Cold War. With old political hostility at an end, it is an unambiguous and shared interest that nuclear stability be achieved between the United States and Russia, and that there should be no counterrevolution against democracy in the new nations of the former Soviet Union. This deep *American* interest in the success of post-Soviet democracy intersects with the American interest in nuclear stability and makes it an easy priority, in the strictest terms of national security, for the U.S. government to help in the process of preventing proliferation and avoiding nuclear accidents as the former Soviet Union becomes a new set of states with nuclear weapons only in Russia.

There are many complexities in this new process. Formidable challenges, both political and technical, lie ahead. Politically, it will be important to create an appropriate cooperative mechanism for material inventory control of the nuclear materials harvested from dismantled weapons; technically, the safe disposal of the highly toxic and potentially threatening stores of plutonium must also receive top priority. But what is most remarkable, so far, is that the effort appears to be strongly supported by public opinion in most of the countries concerned. Such support is justified because it rests in the end on a shared understanding that the achievement of nuclear stability is a shared interest that outweighs inherited concepts of competition and mistrust.

Present circumstances provide a window of opportunity for rapid progress. In addition to the current government-to-government spirit of cooperation, there is currently a broad transparency about activities in the former Soviet Union which eases the burden on formal verification. Increasingly substantive and direct personal contacts between Americans of all sorts and present and former members of the Soviet nuclear and military establishments make it impractical for any successor government to carry out deception on a strategically significant scale. The implementation of START, with its highly intrusive verification regime, can only increase this valuable transparency. Openness does help.

Chapter 2

The Case of Saddam and Other Dangers

THE WORLD'S NUCLEAR DANGER HAS NEVER BEEN limited to the two superpowers. The effort to prevent the spread of nuclear weapons to others has a long history, going back to proposals for international control in 1946. The United States has had misunderstandings with many other countries on this subject. Its efforts to limit the spread of nuclear weapons have been intermittent and uneven; that is true of other major nations too. But the question has acquired a new sharpness because of Saddam Hussein's nuclear weapons program, whose magnitude and meaning were revealed in and after the Gulf War.

The whole story of this secretive Iraqi adventure has not yet been uncovered. What we do know is that for many years, under Saddam, Iraq systematically violated the Non-Proliferation Treaty (NPT) of 1968, which it had signed, by a sustained and secret large-scale program for the purchase or production of everything it might require to make nuclear warheads. Iraqi nuclear ambi-

tion was not a secret before the Gulf War; ten years earlier, in 1981, an Iraqi nuclear installation had been pre-
emptively attacked by Israeli aircraft. It was known in a
number of governments that Iraqi efforts did not stop
after that attack. Early in the Gulf crisis there were official
American warnings of such Iraqi ambition; during the
short combat phase there were American attacks on
Iraqi nuclear installations, and as the war ended the UN
Security Council passed Resolution 687, proclaiming
that this Iraqi effort and others related to weapons of
mass destruction (chemical munitions, missiles) must
stop, and authorizing action to produce that result.

Despite Iraqi efforts to conceal as much as possible, in
the months that followed international inspection teams
gradually exposed a nuclear enterprise of remarkable
breadth and depth. It is now evident that if Saddam's
effort had not been interrupted by the war he provoked, he
would probably have had nuclear weapons sometime in the
1990s—quite possibly in the first half of the decade.
Knowing Saddam as it now does, the world has been
shocked by this narrow escape. It is not surprising that an
effective consensus has developed, growing in strength as
the process of inquiry and dismantling has continued in Iraq,
that the international community should see to it that
leaders such as Saddam do not get the bomb. Saddam
Hussein, by his combination of intense nuclear ambition and
ruthless aggression, has given a wholly new international
priority to the prevention of success in such nuclear programs as his.

These events are too recent to permit a full understanding of the ways and means by which this new priority can produce effective action, but certain things are
clear. It is reasonable to expect that in the case of Iraq
both the investigation and the dismantling of the enterprise

will be carried through with sufficient thoroughness to mean that any renewed Iraqi effort would have to start back near the beginning and would face a continuing prospect of international discovery and response. At least in the short term—say through the 1990s—the world is likely to be spared an Iraqi bomb. The larger and more difficult question is whether the international community can, from this sharply illuminating experience, find the energy and good sense to reexamine and reform the ways and means of its overall effort to ensure that nuclear weapons and ruthless aggressors are kept separate.

In considering this remarkably changed situation it should be noted that the general interest in limiting the number of nuclear-weapon states, and especially in avoiding the case of a Saddam-with-a-bomb, is not intrinsically different from the interest in achieving the most moderate nuclear behavior that is possible between the United States and Russia. A policy designed to prevent additional nuclear-weapon states can seem discriminatory; why do we accept for existing nuclear-weapon states what we are determined to try to prevent for countries like Iraq? In part the argument is simply that in all cases the most moderate nuclear posture that is achievable should be sought; we simply do not know how to get to zero with Americans or Russians, or indeed (as we shall see) with any existing nuclear-weapon state. Yet the example of the dozens of non-nuclear states that have decided against nuclear weapons deserves as much attention as any decision the other way. Keeping the number of nuclear-weapon states as small as possible is in reality a shared interest of all people on earth. There obviously can be powerful motives behind national decisions to seek or to keep nuclear weapons, but a deep *general interest* in an end to nuclear proliferation is shared by *all* states—excepting the few would-be proliferators—whether or not they have nuclear weapons of their own.

TRADITIONAL CONCEPTS OF NONPROLIFERATION

We return to the case of Iraq, and the way to begin is by comparing the present effort to prevent an Iraqi bomb with what was customary before 1991 in efforts to limit proliferation.

The present effort in Iraq rests on a triangular *ad hoc* arrangement. The underlying political authority comes from the continuing support of the UN Security Council; the controlling sanction is the continuing possibility of renewed military action led by the United States; both the discovery by inspection and the verification of dismantling are handled for the Security Council by a Special Commission of its own creation which in nuclear matters relies on inspections conducted with its help by officers of the International Atomic Energy Agency (IAEA), based in Vienna. Without the support of the American military capability at hand and the authority of repeated and specific resolutions of the Security Council, the teams from the IAEA could not be asserting themselves as they are. They also have unusual logistic support and the technical help of experts more numerous and more capable than those ordinarily available.

The need for such special reinforcements is not the fault of the International Atomic Energy Agency. It is a product of the IAEA's origins. The agency was designed in the aftermath of President Eisenhower's initiative called "Atoms for Peace," in the late 1950s. It was to be an agency that would both facilitate and "safeguard" the sharing of nuclear know-how for peaceful purposes. The IAEA, by its charter and by its practice, has *not* been dedicated to the discovery and frustration of secret efforts of sovereign states to obtain what they need for atomic weapons of their own. Rather, it has been dedicated to the application of agreed safeguards to installations announced as engaged in peaceful uses of nuclear materials—usually power reactors. In its relations with non-nuclear states the IAEA has not previously gone beyond the inspection of installations declared as nuclear by the inspected states. Iraq was such a state before 1991, and the installations it declared were not the ones that mattered. The IAEA exercises its responsibilities as an agent of the parties to the NPT; Iraq is such a party, and its secret program was not reached by the "full-scope" safeguards of the NPT. The IAEA, before 1991, was an agency whose jurisdiction and effectiveness were shaped by its origin in an uneasy and mutually wary agreement between those with and those without nuclear weapons; the same limitations applied to the obligations nominally imposed by the NPT. States that agreed not to have nuclear weapons should have access to what they needed for "peaceful uses" of nuclear energy; there should be agreed "safeguards" on installations of this sort. Otherwise there should not be interference with the sovereign rights of either buyers or sellers of exports relevant to nuclear facilities. What is apparent here is the distance that separates the historical purposes of the IAEA and the NPT from the immediate task undertaken by the Security Council in Iraq.

There are other examples of such institutional limitations on the effectiveness of organizations concerned with nuclear danger. The most obvious case is the UN Security Council itself, which can act only if none of its five permanent members is opposed. A still more sweeping requirement of unanimity governs policy decisions by the signatories of the NPT—there a single nation can block any new resolution by voting against it. (Fortunately the question of continuing the NPT will be decided in 1995 by a simple majority.)

There are other important groups of governments, notably the Nuclear Suppliers Group, whose twenty-seven members include most of the states most advanced in the relevant technologies. Its members share a desire to restrict the spread of nuclear weapons, but they also have important commercial interests in exports most of which have legitimate as well as suspect uses—"dual-use items." The Nuclear Suppliers Group has developed increasingly extensive lists of these items, but each member still makes its own decisions on controlling its exports of them. Standards of control and reporting are varied. Furthermore, as technological know-how has spread through the world, the number of suppliers of relevant items has regularly expanded more rapidly than the membership of the Nuclear Suppliers Group.

As it stood before the lesson of Iraq in 1991, the world's antiproliferation regime was rhetorically formidable, but practically porous and permissive. There was essentially nothing necessary for the manufacture of nuclear weapons—no material, no gadget, and no skill or understanding—that could not be acquired with money and without publicity. The speed and accuracy of international detection were low; the effectiveness of international enforcement was lower still.

Certain practical changes are plainly indicated by experience in Iraq. Clearly, for example, the power and capability of the IAEA should be enlarged. In particular the agency should be encouraged by its supporters to exercise—as it did not before Iraq—its power to inspect sites that are *not* reported by member nations as nuclear installations.

Inspections conducted only where they are invited will not protect against a secret program like Saddam's. The IAEA, along with the members of the NPT who have relied upon it, has operated under the presumption that its non-nuclear-weapon members are interested only in plants for the peaceful use of atomic energy and that inspection therefore should be aimed only at the danger of unauthorized diversion of dangerous material from those plants. The power to inspect wherever evidence recommends it does exist, but its use will require a new level of political support from member states, and if necessary from the UN Security Council.

But the question thus presented is much broader. To do a more thorough job the agency will need more staff, with a wider range of skills; it will need support from the large information-collecting services maintained by a number of member states, most notably but not uniquely the United States. It will probably also need the recognized right to announce its findings, support from the UN Security Council, and close and sustained relationships with members of the Nuclear Suppliers Group. Obviously, then, an effective antiproliferation regime will require the support of many countries. The United States may be the most important, if only because some of its intelligence capabilities are unique, and certainly there will be need for American energy in the shared effort, but no one country can do this job.

What is required is a coordinated effort from all the important suppliers, so that judgment and action can be based on a broad range of information, not just haphazard reports. The IAEA must be able to assess the collective meaning of what the suppliers are doing. For the agency to have that level of knowledge, the supplier nations will have to put their interest in this protective effort above their interest in commercial exports. This choice is justified by

treatment from one superpower or both, and those memories are the sharper where the mistreatment came from an ally. The Americans did not give as much help to the British as Franklin Roosevelt had led them to expect. The French received even less help from the Americans and compared it unfavorably to what the British did get. Initial Soviet help to the Chinese is not as well remembered in Beijing as the fact that when relations cooled that help was unceremoniously cut off. It is not surprising that in all these countries decision-makers have been on guard against outside interference with their nuclear-weapon choices.

A central element in their attachment to the bomb has been its importance as a symbol of rank as a great power, to many leaders as important politically as their permanent membership in the UN Security Council. One consequence of this long-standing feeling about *place à table* is that it would probably be a most unpleasant matter for any of the three to sign any arms control agreement in which it formally accepted a lower rank than the Russians and the Americans. It is unlikely that any of them would accept any arrangement under which the number of warheads or launchers or megatons it is allowed is defined as one-third or one-fifth or one-tenth of U.S. and Russian allowances. It is useful here to remember the poisonous political effect among conservatives in Japan of their government's acceptance, in the Washington Naval Treaty of 1920, of a formal ratio of three capital ships to every five for Britain and for the United States. Pride has been a powerful force for Americans and Russians; it should be no surprise to find it strong in the nuclear choices of Britain, France, and China.

Fortunately, it is only an assumption, uncritically drawn from superpower experience, that makes people suppose that formally agreed numerical limits are the only road to moderation and stability in nuclear deployments of these three powers. Their situations are not the same as those of the United States and Russia. Their strategic forces are not designed to be equal to those of someone else. (There may remain some marginal rivalry across the English Channel, but it is hardly decisive in specific procurement decisions; British and French forces are *not* designed to deter one another.) Nor is there any immediate threat to any other country in any of their current deployments or apparent plans for future deployments. This assessment at once suggests what these countries can all do, by their own free choice, to reinforce strategic stability: they can be persuasively open about their present and projected nuclear postures.

It is interesting to consider just what kinds of information it would be constructive for all nuclear-weapon states to share with the world, but there is no need for three Americans to complicate the matter by claiming to know what every other nuclear power should decide to publish. Numbers and yields of warheads come to mind because they are already publicly estimated by a number of independent authorities, and also because they are obviously related to the overall capabilities of any force. But numbers of delivery vehicles—aircraft, missiles, and submarines—are also widely published and also significant. Less often reported, but perhaps more important, are production plans for future forces and prospective retirements of weapons or delivery systems. Broadly speaking, the general interest in all these matters is best served by openness. There remain real and good secrets, for these three powers as for Americans and Russians; they relate mainly to the ways of protecting both the survivability of forces and the means of commanding them.

We all have much to learn about openness, and the best teacher will be experience. There is such a habit of secrecy in *all* nuclear-weapon states that it will take time for each of them to learn that the basic information about what they have and plan to have is not usefully kept secret. Fortunately, there is no need for great haste in this matter. The world knows today the approximate size and shape of British, French, and Chinese forces; it would take very large changes to give any one of these forces a political or military weight significantly different from what it has today, and such changes would be visible with or without openness in the country concerned. Specifically, there is no reason in politics or in logic for reductions in American and Russian forces to be delayed by worries about these three countries until the United States and Russia move well below the level of 3,000 to 3,500 that they now assert will take the rest of the century to reach. Long before that, if current attitudes on these matters continue to change as they have in recent years, both moderation and openness are likely to have more friends in all five countries than they have today.

At the same time, it is well to recognize the probability that Britain, France, and China will not wish to reduce their strategic forces in the same proportion as the two nuclear superpowers are now doing. Each of them, in its own way, believes in a fundamental requirement for a force so clearly able to survive any attack and reply in strength that its existence deters such attack. Starting with much smaller forces, they have less room for reduction than the Americans and the Russians. Just as it may remain hard for a British or French or Chinese government to accept treaty limits explicitly lower than those on the nuclear superpowers, so it may become necessary for Americans and Russians to accept forces in those countries that become *relatively* larger as time passes. Any resistance to such a relative change will be based more on habits of thought than on true national interest. There would be no change in danger, for either nuclear superpower, if one day British or French or Chinese forces, now at less than one-tenth of the superpower level, should each instead become half as large as the two largest forces. And even that remaining difference should reflect national choices, not formally negotiated inequality. If there is continued progress away from nuclear danger, and also a continued increase in the preference now given to conventional forces in the defense budgets of all concerned, the eventual Russian and American responses to such a change, among leaders, experts, and citizens alike, are likely to be untroubled.

Moderation and openness among the other three permanent members of the UN Security Council will have their own value in reinforcing the moderation and openness which we have already urged upon the Big Two, and also in demonstrating that all five permanent members are now prepared to do their part in helping the world turn away from nuclear danger. A readiness to explain what their own forces are and are not intended for—in that sense an acceptance of nuclear accountability—is something that all nuclear powers can contribute to a new worldwide encouragement of continued restraint on the part of those who do *not* try to become nuclear-weapon states. The British, French, and Chinese governments are all important to the process of limiting the spread of nuclear weapons. In the past there have been commercial and political reasons for sales and assistance, as between France and Israel, or China and Pakistan; Americans should not throw stones in either case. In recent years, however, the French and Chinese governments have been less interested in such special relations and more interested in cooperation. In particular both have recently decided to join the Non-Proliferation Treaty. China has been willing to permit the UN Security Council to act firmly in Iraq and is also clearly interested in lowering the threat of a North Korean bomb. Each of the five permanent members has its own way of thinking about nuclear danger and special interests that will be pressed. It is wrong to take it for granted that the five will always be able to cooperate as they have over Iraq. But it is right to insist that there is an urgent need for such cooperation and that it is in the common interest of all five. If they do not all join in supporting a newly effective system of constraint on nuclear-related exports, it is hard to see how such a system can ever be established. There will be a parallel need for five-power participation in ending the production of fissile fuel for warheads.

ISRAEL, INDIA, AND PAKISTAN

The same kind of help is needed, though it may be harder to get, from a less familiar group that can be classified as the unannounced nuclear-weapon states: Israel, India, and Pakistan. It is certain that Israel has a significant stock of warheads and that India has the skills and materials to have warheads as quickly as it wants, and it is highly probable that Pakistan is in a similar situation on a somewhat smaller scale. Their neighbors estimate each of these countries to be a nuclear-weapon state, and we think they are right. In particular India and Pakistan recognize and respect each other's capabilities. The rest of the world would do well to assess these three countries as nuclear-weapon states and to ask of them a greater measure of openness on this subject.

The most important reason for such increased openness from these three countries is the destructive political impact of the pretense that they are not what they are. In different ways each of the three pays a heavy price. The Indians and the Pakistanis have their nuclear programs mainly because of each other—though the Chinese bomb also has weight in New Delhi. The prospect of moderating the nuclear competition between them depends heavily on a shared recognition of their existing capabilities and the grave danger of any expanded competition. There is now some understanding of this situation on both sides, but that understanding will not be strong enough to support agreed constraints on their competition until each of the two countries openly recognizes the other for what it is: a state that has the capability for nuclear weapons, and one that will probably have more such weapons, and new systems of delivery too, if they cannot reach a more moderate arrangement. It is certainly possible that in the search for understanding the two governments could indeed come to recognize that both would be happier if neither had such programs. (Argentina and Brazil made just such a shared decision in 1991, though they had the advantages of holding back at a somewhat earlier stage.) But quite aside from the grave political obstacles to such a shared recognition between two proud and mutually mistrustful states, we must recognize here the difficulty already described in the Russian-American context: Who can ever be sure that a state with nuclear warheads has in reality reduced its supply all the way to zero? What can be hoped for, in the near term, is that India and Pakistan can find a way to act on the reality that the best course for both is to find the ways and means toward cooperative reduction in their nuclear-weapon postures. To do that they must begin from where they are.

Israel—along with her well-known friend the United States—suffers from what looks to other countries in the region like a hypocritical deception, but the Israelis face great difficulties in the open recognition of reality. They have an elaborate pretense that they are reluctant to abandon. Many of them argue that a secret program gives less pain to their neighbors, and probably they also do not wish to trouble any friends (especially in the United States) for whom a declared Israeli bomb would be embarrassing. Their pretense grows thinner as public debate about their nuclear capability becomes more candid. The number of those outside Israel who are comforted by the pretense shrinks, and the number who find it absurd and even offensive grows. The pretense prevents any public defense of the Israeli program by the Israeli government and any effective argument that no state or group need fear an Israeli bomb unless it attempts the destruction of Israel.

The official American view of the Israeli bomb is a somewhat separate subject. The American government has never publicly supported the Israeli nuclear program, although no American administration ever used all the influence it might have to obstruct it. We shall never know whether an American denial of other kinds of assistance could have changed Israeli nuclear policy, because the Americans never used that power with determination. Today the American government could say in public that along with all other well-informed observers it considers Israel to be a nuclear-weapon state. Such a statement would clarify an important reality, follow the guideline of openness, and help the Israelis themselves to tell the truth. The trouble with this course of action is that in nuclear matters even more than others, countries do not like their secrets to be told by others (though this one is now only nominally a secret). A further trouble is that proud, small countries hate to be corrected by large friends. The best way out of this cul-de-sac is Israeli openness by Israeli decision. Americans in and out of government can properly urge such an Israeli choice.

The advantage of recognizing Israel, India, and Pakistan for what they are is not merely a matter of dealing with reality, important though that is. It is also a matter of *not* dealing with these countries as they are *not*. One cannot make much sense in talking about nuclear restraint in the Middle East if one omits the existence of Israeli warheads.

It also makes little sense to try to respond to the dangers of the Indian subcontinent as if there were still some way in which outside influence could keep it nonnuclear. Outside influence was feeble, and it failed. Given the size and sophistication of the countries concerned, the depth of their differences, the certainty that one would follow the other, and the fact that each had powerful friends, it is not at all clear that the subcontinent could ever have been brought to take a different course. Certainly it is too late now. It remains prudent for outsiders not to encourage or assist the effort of either country, but if India and Pakistan are to put effective limits to the danger in their competition, they will now have to do it, in the first instance, as nuclear-weapon states dealing directly with each other.

As with the five holders of larger arsenals, so for India, Pakistan, and Israel there is good sense in moderation as well as openness. All three wanted the bomb for deeply defensive reasons—to deter or repel a possible mortal assault on their own land. There may be differences of opinion in other capitals on the gravity of the threat faced by these countries, but what their neighbors should understand is that for each of the three, in its own way, the bomb is a *defensive* weapon. Openness about their defensive reasons for possessing nuclear arms can be helpful in limiting fearful responses of others. Openness will also permit them to play a more constructive role in efforts against proliferation. While none of them has the operational importance, for general worldwide nonproliferation policy, that accompanies permanent membership and veto power in the Security Council, none of these three states is trivial in its weight on this wider front. Each has friends that will respect its voice on this subject, and none has any national interest whatsoever in encouraging any irresponsible proliferator. The fact that these three countries are quiet about their nuclear capabilities is a form of moderation that deserves some respect. Whatever makes them believe they need such weapons, it is not mere vanity and still less an indication of aggressive threat.

Nonetheless it is best to describe them as they are— nuclear-weapon states. Not to do so is to pretend, and pretense is the enemy of understanding. Nor should this recognition of reality be avoided on the ground that it would confer political prestige on these states. Instead it is time for recognition that it makes no sense to think of nuclear weapons as merit badges. In today's climate, when it is clear that there is a worldwide turn away from nuclear danger, it may in fact be more fashionable not to have nuclear weapons than to have them. The sensible course for all countries is moderation, and each country must be moderate from where it really is, not from some pretended position. If the pretense is maintained that these three states are not nuclear-weapon states, then all that can be expected over the next few years is the gradual erosion of that pretense, and with it a growing sense that the race against proliferation is somehow being lost. If instead the attentive world describes these countries as they are, then there is a good chance that they too can have policies that help to reduce the level of existing nuclear danger. Like other nuclear-weapon states they too can be more moderate, more open, less threatening, more careful, in the future than in the past.

Yet a further difficulty is presented by the nuclear-weapon reality in these three states. They belong to a class—nuclear-weapon states that did not test a nuclear device before 1967—that does not exist in the Non-Proliferation Treaty. Unless the treaty is amended—itself a difficult and uncertain process—these three countries cannot be members. It is probably fortunate, given present reality, that none of them ever joined back in early years: at least they are not in unconfessed violation of the treaty. The difficulty is more a matter of form than of reality, because it remains entirely practicable for these three countries to be as firm in avoiding help to would-be proliferators as the most ardent member of the NPT, and they should be encouraged in such a course.

STATES THAT DO NOT HAVE NUCLEAR WEAPONS AND DO NOT WANT THEM

It is comforting to turn from the difficult and still cloudy position of the unannounced nuclear-weapon states to what may be the most neglected and the largest class of nations: those that have firmly decided against nuclear weapons. They are different in all sorts of ways, but together they constitute a powerful reinforcement to the worldwide effort to limit or even end nuclear spread. This reinforcement comes not only from their existence but also from the variety of the reasons for their non-nuclear positions.

Consider some notable cases. The Germans and the Japanese have stayed clear of nuclear weapons first because they were required to do so as losers in World War II, but secondly, and much more deeply, because they do not see this kind of apocalyptic strength as desirable in terms of their basic political relations with their neighbors. In a different way, and even earlier, the Canadians decided not to continue and expand what they had done as junior partners in the work that led to the first American bomb; a weapon so expensive and destructive simply did not fit their own view of their defense requirements. The Mexicans were never interested, and Americans who are occasionally irritated by Mexican criticism (as of U.S. testing) should remember how much better it is to have a critical neighbor than a nearby nuclear rival. The Swedes had a nuclear-research program that some of their defense officials would have expanded, precisely as a modern protector of their traditional neutrality, but the final political decision went against that choice. Except for Britain and France, all other Western Europeans held back. So did all of South America and most of Africa. In Argentina and Brazil enthusiasts for nuclear weapons, in a mutually reinforcing rivalry, came close to the nuclear brink before cooler political heads prevailed. South Korea and Taiwan once had nuclear ambitions, but over time both reached a negative judgment. South Africa went further and learned how to make a bomb, but in 1992 its government turned back.

South Africa's record is unique; it has made six nuclear devices and then dismantled them all. South Africa's change of policy led to her accession to the Non-Proliferation Treaty and acceptance of international safeguards. On March 24, 1993, Prime Minister De

Klerk made a remarkable speech explaining South Africa's record, and expressing the hope that its initiative "will inspire other countries to take the same steps." It is a fair challenge.

The full roll cannot be called here, but it is evident that most countries do *not* seek nuclear weapons and have their own good reasons to support worldwide nuclear moderation, so that in a deep sense there is not a division between nuclear-weapon and most non-nuclear-weapon states. The historical reasons for international arrangements based on this division are less important than they once were, and some traditional antipathies are becoming out-of-date. The true line of division is between the vast majority of all states, on the one hand, and the very small number that are now actively but covertly attempting to get the bomb for themselves.

Any careful list of the states in this latter category would include Iraq, Iran, North Korea, and Libya. A few countries that have turned away from past ambition, such as South Africa, Argentina, and Brazil, also present problems because of supplies and capabilities left over from earlier times. Such a list is neither exhaustive nor definitive, but it does suggest that in the coming decade it will make sense to think about nuclear proliferation not only in terms of the general effectiveness of the international nonproliferation regime but also in terms of the kinds of actions most likely to affect the choices of the particular countries with present nuclear-weapon ambitions.

That leaves a lot to be done. The need for major reinforcement of the relevant international agencies has already been noted. International pressure or responsiveness, or both, can also be valuable in particular situations. It is also important to work region by region, when that is what is acceptable, as in the creation of

regional nuclear-free zones. Iraq is a case where pressure—including intense military action—has been successful. It also appears that recent moderation in
Argentina and Brazil has been encouraged by the
regional Treaty of Tlateloco—more acceptable to these two
countries than the Non-Proliferation Treaty, which neither
has joined.

The most troubling case today may be that of North
Korea. On the one hand there appears to be a new
urgency in the concerns of all of North Korea's neighbors including Russia, China, Japan, and the United
States through its presence in South Korea. On the other
hand the government of North Korea seems determined to
protect its nuclear-weapon effort by preventing inspection
and threatening withdrawal from the NPT. If such
intransigence is maintained or repeated (the North
Korean regime is experienced in cat-and-mouse games), the
readiness of the permanent members of the Security
Council to enforce inspection on North Korea as they
have on Iraq will be tested.

But pragmatic standards must be applied in reinforcing such complex and imperfect institutions as the
UN Security Council, the NPT, the IAEA, and the
Nuclear Suppliers Group. The imperfections of these
institutions are not, for the most part, accidental. They
reflect the preferences—at least the one-time preferences—of important participants, and they will not be
changed dramatically by the desire of a single nation.
Nonetheless the United States should generally encourage
the strengthening of all these multilateral institutions,
and it should recognize that two primary requirements for
such a change are the readiness of the over-armed Americans for sustained reduction in their own nuclear forces
and the readiness of the rich Americans to take a fair

part in financing effective international agencies. In terms of real national interest, this is not a contest between haves and have-nots; it is a matter of varied contributions to achieving a shared objective.

Most countries, varied as they are in their attitudes toward the possession of nuclear weapons of their own, have it in common that they have no reason to support the spread of nuclear weapons beyond the eight countries that should now be counted as having them. In certain cases in the past a country may have put the cause of nonproliferation second to a more immediate political or economic interest. Looking back, most countries—the United States is one—are usually not proud of such choices. Looking forward, it is clear that the common interest in avoiding Saddamite bombs outweighs narrow interests in nuclear sales and should no longer yield to any Cold War interest in helping a regional friend. The special priorities of the past, visible for example in the record of American policy toward Israel and Pakistan, need not be a part of future behavior by any of the countries capable of relevant sales and assistance. In terms of their own true national interests, all countries but the few with present nuclear ambition can be hoped for as effective supporters of a new international regime that reaffirms and effectively supports a worldwide policy of preventing the spread of nuclear weapons.

Chapter 3

Putting It Together in Washington

A S AMERICANS ADDRESSING IN THE FIRST INSTANCE OUR fellow citizens, we arrive in this last chapter at the question that belongs to us all by the basic rules of our society: what should we ask of our national government in its policy and behavior with respect to nuclear danger? We have already made many points that bear on this question, but we ourselves learned a lot by asking ourselves quite specifically what present worldwide conditions tell us about what our own government should try to achieve in 1993 and thereafter. That inquiry led to ten propositions that we think important for American policy.

1. The United States should respect the reality that as long as there are nuclear bombs, there will be a danger that is unique in all history.

We have seen that the bomb is uniquely dangerous because it is uniquely destructive—so destructive that in all the conflict and tumult of the long Cold War no one chose to use it, or to provoke its use by others. That reality must permeate American policy choices even more thoroughly in the future than in the past. It requires respect and honor to those who have shown responsible control over these weapons. It also requires, at the other end of policy-making, a higher priority than ever for choices that can help to prevent the possession of this weapon by international adventurers like Saddam Hussein. Respect for nuclear danger is a guiding element in all the remaining propositions of this chapter.

2. The United States should seek wider and deeper understanding on nuclear danger with as many other governments as possible, beginning with the other nuclear-weapon states.

Such understanding is at once the best protection against the danger of large-scale nuclear warfare and a necessary element in worldwide nuclear restraint. The most impressive demonstration of this broad proposition lies in the reality of what Americans and Russians have achieved—together with many others—in ending the Cold War. Underlying the great new Russian-American arms-control measures of the last two years, and giving promise of further progress, is a set of interlocking political decisions and actions that have turned the Russians and the Americans from opponents to friends. Their nuclear competition now has no cause but itself, and both sides, in their actions of the last few years, have shown their understanding that all they need from these weapons, with respect to each other, is clear assurance that neither side will ever be able to achieve, without ample notice, any nuclear advantage that might be considered usable against the other. As we have seen, there is no short road to complete nuclear disarmament, but the road away from superpower confrontation has indeed been opened; the United States and Russia can walk that road together, to their common advantage, as they learn together the arts of cooperative nuclear moderation, under START I and II and the exchanged announcements of major tactical reductions.

Also important for the long run, and less often remembered, is the absence of underlying political hostility between the United States and all other announced nuclear-weapon states. The United States does not think of any of them as potential enemies in war—not the British or the French, self-evidently; not the Chinese because both countries have learned better over the forty years since Korea. Only China has ever been a possible opponent in nuclear war, and the case deserves notice.

There was a danger of American nuclear action against China during the last months of the Korean war in 1953, and another such danger during the two crises over Quemoy and Matsu a few years later. The degree of the danger in these two cases is far from clear, but there is no doubt that each time both governments found themselves thinking about the possibility of American warheads falling on Chinese targets. The difference, four decades later, is that neither side now sees the other as a remotely likely enemy in nuclear war. The historical and geopolitical reasons for this change are numerous. They include the Vietnam war, in which the two countries carefully avoided direct conflict, the opening to China by President Nixon, and the complex coexistence of the last twenty years. The remaining differences between the two countries in the 1990s are not trivial, but they do not come near the level of military conflict. The absence of direct hostility between China and the United States does not make that relationship the same, in other ways, as American relations with England, France, or even

Russia, but it does mean that the nuclear danger between them that both have felt in the past no longer exists. Other differences with China persist, but it makes no sense for either side to let those differences prevent a cooperation against nuclear danger.

More broadly, Americans can expect differences with all of the four other permanent members of the Security Council, but not warfare with any. The political changes required to alter this expectation are very large, and there would be plenty of time for any necessary American response in either conventional or nuclear rearmament before such changes could have a direct impact on nuclear balance or nuclear danger. The prudent judgment for the present is that it should be both the American purpose and the American expectation that in the 1990s the five permanent members should continue on their new course of cooperation against nuclear danger. In these matters they are not in hot competition, and there is no underlying political animosity that need prevent them from working together. Pride is another matter; so is greed; so is misunderstanding. Any one of the three can hamper or even prevent cooperation. But the common real interest is to work together against nuclear danger.

The same general rule applies to our nuclear-danger relations with all other countries. Except for a few—perhaps Iraq, Iran, North Korea, and Libya—all the world's governments now favor an end to nuclear proliferation. What is true of the five announced nuclear-weapon states is true of the three other states that must be judged to have nuclear warheads of their own: Israel, India and Pakistan. Their formal status is a question of some difficulty, but neither their neighbors nor the world can doubt that, in terms of what they could do in desperation, they are nuclear-weapon states. Still they are not eager for nuclear competition or open threat, let alone for aggressive use of what they have. They can join in reducing their own contribution to nuclear danger.

Still more clearly on the side of reducing nuclear danger are the scores of states, large and small, that have definitely rejected the course of obtaining their own nuclear weapons. The basic division in the world on the subject of nuclear proliferation is not between those with and without nuclear weapons. It is between almost all nations and the very few who currently seek weapons to reinforce their expansive ambition.

3. American first use of nuclear weapons should be governed by a stringent doctrine of defensive last resort.

The United States should make it plain that the overriding purpose of having nuclear weapons is to avoid their use, not only by others against the United States but also by the United States against anyone else. The United States should recognize the great costs of any break in the worldwide tradition of nonuse, and take care to attend to its interests, as far as it can, by other capabilities. As matters now stand, every vital interest of the United States, with the exception of deterring nuclear attack, can be met by prudent conventional readiness; there is no visible case where the United States could be forced to choose between defeat and the first use of nuclear weapons. This is one crucial consequence of the transformation of Europe since 1989. For as far ahead as we can now see, the American president will be able to accompany support for a doctrine of defensive last resort with the assurance that he sees no present likelihood of any confrontation that would require this dreadful choice. Indeed the U.S. government has already gone a long way in this direction. A doctrine of last

resort was adopted by NATO in 1991, and in the
NATO context the word "defensive" can fairly be taken
for granted—by its own language the North Atlantic
Treaty is a defensive alliance. This new NATO doctrine
gives reassurance of both support and prudence to all
members. It can do the same thing more broadly as a
basic doctrine of the United States.

Both nuclear history and present nuclear politics
would support a doctrine one step more rigid—a doctrine that nuclear weapons should be used only in
response to their use by others—commonly called no-
first-use. This is the posture that was urged by some for
NATO when the dominant opinion was that only a
readiness for first use would ensure against communist
aggression.[1] President Carter moved toward this posture
when he declared in 1978 that the United States would
never use nuclear weapons against a non-nuclear-
weapon state unless it was acting as the ally of a state
with nuclear weapons. The last clause was aimed at the possible case of an aggressive ally of the Soviet Union; the case
lively in memory was that of North Korea from 1950 to
1953. The clear priority for American military planners
today is to keep their present capability to deter or
defeat a conventional aggressor by conventional means.
There is no early danger that this capability will be lost, so
our present leaders should reaffirm the 1978 assurance;
indeed, taking account of the end of the Cold War, they can
strengthen it. There is no present obstacle to an American
declaration against *any* use of nuclear weapons against a
non-nuclear-weapon state.

---

[1] See, for example, McGeorge Bundy, George F. Kennan, Robert S.
McNamara and Gerard Smith, "Nuclear Weapons and the Atlantic
Alliance," *Foreign Affairs*, Spring 1982.

In recognizing the possibility of a future case in which there might be justification for a use of nuclear weapons as a defensive last resort, we are simply resisting the notion that our country can be certain *a priori* that there will never be a case when such use might be the least bad choice. The steady policy of the United States should be to do its part, by arms control, conventional capability, and the general worldwide reduction of nuclear danger, to ensure that no such terrible choice ever becomes necessary. All of these lines of action can and should be pursued under a doctrine of defensive last resort.

The doctrine of defensive last resort has one further advantage. It corresponds to the nuclear policy of other nuclear-weapon states much more closely than a flat policy of no-first-use. We have already noted that Russian possession of nuclear weapons helps to give the Russians confidence that they do not endanger their homeland when they accept the independence of Eastern Europe and the break-up of the Soviet Union. As long as the Russians have the bomb, there is little danger of large-scale attack by others on Russia for the decisive reason that no one could expect them to accept any large defeat without resort to the bomb. In 1982 Brezhnev affirmed a policy of no-first-use, but that doctrine was clearly designed to moderate superpower nuclear rivalry; no one contemplating war with Russia would now read it to mean that the Russians would in fact accept serious defeat on their own land without resort to any weapon at hand. There is a parallel protection for France in its nuclear capability; without it Paris might be deeply uncomfortable with its larger but bomb-free German neighbor. Britain's position is less clear-cut, because the surrounding seas protect it from those nearby and because the possible threat from Russia is not only distant, but more nuclear than conventional—requiring defense by deterrence, not by a last resort to first use.

But it is not surprising that among all the permanent members of the Security Council only China has declared an unqualified policy of no-first-use. The Chinese have become confident, after conflicts with Soviets, Americans, Indians, and Vietnamese, that they can hold their own against all possible opponents without resort to nuclear weapons except as a deterrent to the nuclear weapons of others. If Americans had only themselves to defend they could make a parallel declaration; no one is going to threaten the United States conventionally on its own territory. But as it is, with contingent obligations overseas and friends who still rely in some measure on its nuclear protection, and with other nuclear powers sharing its caution for their own reasons, it makes sense for the United States to have a doctrine one step broader—a doctrine of defensive last resort.

This doctrine also fits the requirements of the three unannounced nuclear-weapon states—Israel, India, and Pakistan. The Israeli case is the clearest: the underlying motivation for the Israeli bomb is clearly the reality of vastly outnumbering unfriendly neighbors. The fact that the Israeli bomb is not for casual use is evident both in the desperate conventional battles that have been fought without its use and in the intense Israeli commitment to conventional strength. Evidence on Indian and Pakistani policy is thinner, but the general weight of informed judgment is that each country is governed more by fear than by ambition, and that each feels its nuclear need primarily because of perceived danger from the other. In this situation the immediately urgent requirement is to reduce the level of tension between the two; the first contribution that nuclear policy can make is that of mutually recognized moderation in weapons development and deployment. Sharing in the worldwide adoption of a doctrine of defensive last resort could be helpful here.

To recognize the possibility that in some future defense against aggression the use of the nuclear weapon could unexpectedly become the only alternative to an even worse disaster is not to encourage reliance by planners on any such action, nor does it support any doctrine of early use. A doctrine of defensive last resort is fully consistent with a continuing American effort to sustain the worldwide tradition of nonuse. Indeed, the American interest in a worldwide effort against any use of nuclear weapons is clear and strong, and it is equally clear that it will take visible American leadership to ensure such an effort.

4. American budgetary priorities in action against nuclear danger should be shifted away from our nuclear deployments to support cooperative reduction with Russia, full acceptance of non-nuclear status by other successor states like Ukraine, and reinforced international action to prevent further proliferation around the world.

The United States should think about all its national actions affecting nuclear danger with a recognition that there is no *a priori* reason to prefer arms to arms control, or action by agreement to independent choice. What is essential is to understand the particular advantages and disadvantages of particular choices and act accordingly.

In the 1990s a particularly interesting set of choices is forced upon those who determine the priorities of the defense budget. The defining reality here is a national conviction that the end of the Cold War both permits and demands a change in national budgetary priorities. The downward pressure this conviction creates is powerfully reinforced by two other interlocking requirements: the need to attend to other national priorities usually considered "domestic," and the even broader need to increase national investment and decrease national fiscal irresponsibility. These needs must be addressed, but it makes sense to keep room, as a matter of the most elemental national defense priority, for a financially solid program of reducing nuclear danger.

Of the four elements that define such a program, the first two fall largely outside the direct concern of this book; fortunately they already have broad political support. They are the reduction of the overall defense budget and the shift of financial priorities within that budget toward conventional and away from nuclear forces.

Our own analysis strongly supports such a shift in the overall nuclear/conventional balance. A worldwide American policy of nuclear reduction, nonproliferation, and reduced reliance on any early nuclear use is simply not consistent with large-scale American efforts to expand the role of nuclear weapons. If the United States needs weapons that are more effective or more precise than its best present conventional systems and its smallest tactical nuclear warheads, it should seek them on the conventional side of the line.

During the Cold War Americans thought the best way to reduce the nuclear danger from the Soviet Union was by a fully matching set of nuclear developments and deployments. Now the best way is cooperation, and many actions already taken show that this point is increasingly understood. Both Congress and the Bush administration took remarkable steps in this direction. The Congress, by the Nunn-Lugar Amendment, assigned $400 million a year, in the defense budgets for 1992 and 1993, to the task of assisting a nuclear-weapons clean-up in the former Soviet Union. The executive branch in 1992 agreed to purchase up to five hundred tons of Russian enriched weapons-grade uranium. These actions had general bipartisan support, demonstrating that there was wide understanding of their contributions not only to arms reductions but to the national security of the United States. They should also be seen as first steps towards further cooperation, by all the nuclear-capable states, to limit the supply and control the diffusion of fissionable material.

The need for action of this sort will continue and expand. American readiness to help will strengthen the hands of all those in Russia and other successor states who prefer the turn against nuclear danger to any more adventurous course. Moreover, actions of this kind, insofar as they provide American dollars for activities in the common interest of reducing nuclear danger, are also a general reinforcement to the economy of Russia and other affected states, and therefore serve the broader American interest in the political success of moderate, democratic governments.

There is a parallel value in strengthening international arrangements for limiting nuclear proliferation. If agencies such as IAEA are to have wider responsibilities and powers in this field, American reinforcement will be essential, since both habit and interest will produce strong demands from other states that if IAEA is to be stronger in enforcement it must also be stronger in its work for cooperation in peaceful nuclear uses. If there is to be reinforcement of the flow of information about trade in relevant materials and devices, there must also be reinforcement of the primary source—American intelligence—and indeed such reinforcement has begun.

There is a complex question about the possible future role of a separate agency of the Security Council, functioning like the special commission that has been necessary in the case of Iraq. It is not clear that IAEA, with its inherited ethos of trust in those it monitors, can do all the hard work alone.

If there is to be timely international action against suspect states, the Security Council must be ready to act, and here American support will be crucial. When there is also need for a UN force, it will help greatly if there is a new American readiness to participate.

If there is to be effective regional action that encourages restraint and penalizes its opposite, in most cases the United States must be ready to share in such action. More generally, as the case of Saddam clearly illustrates, the power that backs up any insistence on unwelcome inspection is likely to be insufficient unless the Americans are visibly able and ready to help. Fortunately it is probable that very few cases will be as sharp as that of Saddam.

Largely missing so far on the American scene, and greatly needed, is a major effort, including leaders from both parties, to make it clear, especially to our own people, that American help of this kind is indeed a matter of attending to *nuclear danger,* just as much as any direct payment for American nuclear weapons systems. The funds for such work should be considered as a part of a national budget against nuclear danger. Treating them in this way will make clear not only what they are for but how moderate they are in comparison to the sums the United States will still be spending on nuclear weapons systems even as such forces are reduced.

5. The United States should join with all other interested states in a comprehensive test ban treaty.

The problem of nuclear testing presents both an obvious opportunity and a somewhat less obvious difficulty for the United States. The comprehensive test ban has been debated for more than thirty years. In principle the United States was for it, but in practice the Cold War produced nuclear fear and competitiveness that prevented agreement. Now, with the end of the Cold War and the beginning of nuclear moderation, the United States does not need tests for new warheads with either larger or smaller capabilities than those it now has. America's present large-yield warheads are quite destructive enough, and at the lower end of the scale it would be better to seek conventional weapons with improved accuracy and penetration. It is excellent that the Bush administration in 1992 ruled out nuclear weapons tests for new designs, and it is wrong for anyone to encourage the nuclear-weapons laboratories to seek support for such designs, except for safety improvements. Programs of this kind, indeed, would sharply weaken the American effort to reduce nuclear danger. They would make it plain to the rest of the world that the U.S. policy of reduced reliance on nuclear forces was for export only.

In this situation the most important past arguments against a comprehensive treaty fade, and the historic arguments in its favor come to the fore: it will help limit the spread of weapons; it will help dampen the competition among those who already have warheads.

More generally, the end of testing has been an asserted objective of all members of the Non-Proliferation Treaty for almost twenty-five years. In that time, the United States, which has always found reasons of one sort or another for resisting a ban, has come to be perceived as deliberately hostile to an objective it accepted in 1968 as part of the bargain struck between states with and without nuclear weapons in the NPT. There is therefore a considerable political cost in any continued American opposition to a comprehensive test ban.

For all these reasons we have supported the U.S. policy that began to emerge in 1992: a phased approach to an internationally agreed end of testing during this decade, an approach that permits a limited number of tests in the 1990s, with the primary objective of safety. In this period overall safety will also be improved if the deep reductions of START II are carried out as scheduled, because many present safety concerns center on warheads that will be retired in these reductions; in this sense nuclear-arms reduction is itself a contributor to weapon safety.

It may well be true, as partisans of testing often argue, that American testing is not a cause of nuclear ambition in a leader like Saddam Hussein; such leaders will want the bomb, if they can get it, with or without American underground tests. But the argument misses the real point: many people in many countries, who are strong believers in a common effort against nuclear danger, have learned over a long period to put a test ban high on their list of priorities, and to measure the seriousness of the nuclear-weapon states by their readiness to support such a ban. The United States does not need new nuclear capabilities, and its support for a nuclear test ban would strengthen its position among people whose help it needs. The case seems clear.

Still, on technical grounds alone, a limited and temporary exception for safety testing makes sense. The safety of nuclear weapons is a common interest of all states, and since we cannot expect an early end to the current stockpiles—only their steady and sober reduction—limited safety testing is justified to reduce real concerns about warheads remaining in the stockpile. We have believed that a limited and temporary exception for underground safety testing would not seriously affect the prospects for a comprehensive test ban treaty.

There is also no harm in some sharing of increased understanding of the safety problem, and no grave danger in the associated sharing of some other elements of weapons technology. By now there are few real secrets to protect, and there are also experts from a number of nations who could be trusted to monitor such tests without sharing any other technological information they obtain with proliferators. Monitoring of safety tests would be only a forerunner of the extensive and genuinely international process that will be required to verify worldwide compliance with a nonproliferation regime that includes a comprehensive test ban treaty.

The need for safety tests is not good news for those who have both a deep commitment to early achievement of a complete test ban and a long experience of delays defended on the ground that there was this or that continued justification for testing. But the reality is that some American weapons are not as safe as they could and should be. They can be made properly safe, but not without some time and some tests. While the 1996 cutoff mandated by Congress in 1992 does not hold if a foreign state tests after that date, it was a reasonable deadline for American safety testing. The passage of this conditional test-ban legislation was a landmark showing the new post–Cold War priorities of the American government.

Yet we do not believe that the need for safety testing is so urgent or compelling that it should override all other objectives. The importance and desirability of resuming testing has to be weighed against informed political judgment of the value of strengthening and even preserving a nonproliferation regime if the current de facto moratorium on testing is continued. It may be also that our initial judgment that limited U.S. safety testing would have only limited impact on others was too optimistic.

An early comprehensive test ban treaty would indeed be a great achievement, marking the end of almost two thousand tests spanning half a century. It could well be decisive in opening the road to a reaffirmed and reinforced worldwide nonproliferation regime in 1995, and the early achievement of such a regime is more important to worldwide nuclear safety than further improvement in the safety of part of the U.S. nuclear force.

Broad considerations like these led President Clinton to the decision he announced on July 3, 1993, that at least until September 1994 the United States will continue its moratorium on all nuclear tests, unless others begin testing. We note that the question of the political effect of American choices on the choices of other relevant states is one that can be judged best by those who have responsibility in Washington. In the end, as we have all three learned from direct experience, choices of this kind are properly and inescapably presidential. We strongly support President Clinton's decision.

A comprehensive test ban extending over generations would entail a gradual erosion of confidence in the reliability of remaining nuclear warheads. (Reliability in this context means dependable explosion on command; it is not the same as warhead safety.) This would present new issues, and the proper response will depend on the degree of progress that has been made by then in reducing both nuclear danger and the traditional reliance on nuclear deterrence of high technical precision.

The central point remains. The congressional action of 1992 and President Clinton's action of 1993 have laid the basis for American leadership in reaching a comprehensive test-ban treaty. Such a treaty, much more than a fragile moratorium, will weigh against proliferation, and indeed against enlargement of nuclear arsenals.

6. *Americans should respect the scientific and techno-logical realities of nuclear danger, as in choices about strategic defense.*

In the effort to reduce nuclear danger there is a recurrent tendency to ask more of technical experts than nature permits—to make us safe, by science and technology, from what science and technology have made possible. Sometimes technological enthusiasts contribute to the confusion by advertising more than they can deliver. The case that is currently relevant is that of strategic defense. There really is no prospect at all that all-out defense can outrun all-out offense in nuclear warfare, because of the deep but simple reality with which this report began: the overwhelming destructiveness of every single nuclear warhead. A kill-rate of even 10 percent will provide effective defense against ordinary bombers attacking with ordinary bombs: the largest bomber force will fade in a month of such continued attrition. But with nuclear warheads arriving on ballistic missiles, a kill-rate of 90 percent—extraordinarily hard to achieve—is wholly inadequate. Even 95 percent is not enough: for the smallest American and Russian forces in sight for the end of the century, it could mean some 150 warheads on homeland targets. And no one is now proposing that any defensive force of this quality is possible by any technology at all.

Once overall strategic defense is put aside as impossible—which in reality is what the U.S. government has already done in the last two years—the question of what should be done can be addressed more realistically.

The United States can keep a sharp eye out for some real possibility of a technical revolution between strategic offense and defense; prudence requires no less, and the United States should not allow its bad experience with the Strategic Defense Initiative (SDI), as originally advertised, to make it imprudently inattentive. It can also sustain an active and flexible program, consistent with the Antiballistic Missile (ABM) Treaty of 1972, on the less difficult but still demanding mission of defense against limited strikes. In regional conflicts such defenses can have both practical and psychological value against missiles with less-than-nuclear warheads, and the development and production of such systems can proceed in accord with the ABM Treaty. There are still many outstanding questions about the potential effectiveness of nationwide defenses against only one or a few nuclear-armed missiles of intercontinental range launched, perhaps, accidentally. These questions can be addressed by a treaty-consistent research program. But effective defense against a large force of nuclear-armed missiles would require a wholly different level of effectiveness, simply because of the requirement of a kill-rate near 100 percent. A gulf of ignorance and uncertainty still separates the United States from any prospect of a defensive capability that would make it useful to seek a change in the ABM Treaty. It is important to remember that a basic principle undergirding the strategic reductions of recent years is that any nation remains inescapably vulnerable to a large-scale attack. It is hard to accept this reality, but not so hard to see that all one can get from imperfect defense is the same situation with multiplied costs and fears.

7. Stable moderation should not be disturbed by the traditional claims of traditional strategic targeting.

One of the problems that has been overtaken by the new Russian-American agreements is that of targeting. The reduced forces now in prospect will certainly not fit the targeting plans or doctrines of the past, but there is no harm in that, because the process of targeting for nuclear-war-winning is no longer needed in an age in which there is no Cold War and no surviving belief in winning a strategic nuclear war. Responsible targeting officers have always been able to make full use of available forces in their plans, but it is simply not true that smaller plans with smaller forces will be inadequate for strategic deterrence. The possibility of even a few nuclear detonations in populated areas provides ample deterrence, and targeting staff should be able to make plans that produce this result against many different target sets with forces much smaller than those now in prospect. Of course targets will be different at these lower levels. The Strategic Command can be expected to continue to move away from reliance on a single integrated operational plan toward capability for action tailored as closely as possible to specific situations. Two examples of U.S. nuclear action against Russia that remain theoretically possible are the case of a reply to some Russian first use of nuclear weapons and the case of defensive last resort against a conventional assault on Western Europe; each of these unlikely cases would require a most carefully considered choice of targets. There are many complexities in the process of planning for any nuclear strike that lie beyond the scope of this analysis. However, professionals in the targeting staff can ensure that stable strategic deterrence is alive and well at all the reduced levels of strategic strength that are otherwise achievable. The Single Integrated Operational Plan (SIOP) of earlier decades may be dead, but it need not be mourned.

The problem of targeting, in the Cold War years, was perhaps the clearest single example of the damage done by attempts to apply to nuclear weapons the ordinary standards of military analysis. Conversely, the end of the Cold War is permitting a general recognition and acceptance of a better view. At the beginning of the nuclear competition, given the perception of a single-minded and implacably hostile adversary and the assumption that the bomb, for all its power, was best understood simply as one more weapon, it was understandable that commanders should make plans for a winning strategic strike. The requirements for such a capability were destructive power, speed of delivery, accuracy, and an interlocking process of massive attack in which any defenses would be taken out by a first wave of warheads to open the way for the main attack, while any mobile targets would be pursued and destroyed by manned bombers that could hunt them down. Similar standards of war-fighting capability were applied in preparing to defend U.S. strategic submarines and attack those of the enemy. The United States had to plan to do all these things not only because it was aiming at victory but because the adversary was doing similar things and must never be allowed to succeed.

In the years of Gorbachev and Reagan this long and strenuous competition was overtaken by understanding and action based on two realities. First, the technological reality of nuclear attack and defense did not permit either side to expect any outcome but general disaster in a full-scale nuclear war between the two; second, the reality of politics was that the two superpowers were no longer enemies, and indeed could now be friends. Each of these realities helped in understanding the other, and together they undermined the inherited assumptions of strategic commanders and targeters. There is now no need to plan for full-scale strategic warfare because neither side wants such a war, and because in such a war both sides would be ghastly losers. It is their understanding of these realities that permits military professionals to support the reductions of START I and II.

The earlier tradition of strategic targeting, protected by intense secrecy, and much prized as an argument for preserving and modernizing this or that weapons system of this or that service, had a longer life than it deserved. The reality that a general nuclear war would have no winners was already clear to strategic commanders in the 1970s. The 1990s have brought the further technological lesson that no generally effective defense is available and the deep political lesson that continued strategic competition is unnecessary: both sides *can* stop. Both *can* cut back together, and that is what best serves the interests of both.

Nothing illustrates this evolution more clearly, on the American side, than the story of the American MX-missile. It was a first-strike weapon in its conception, designed to deliver ten warheads on ten targets before any opponent could knock it out. It was the preferred new weapon of the air force in the 1970s and early 1980s, defended by one budget compromise after another, and perhaps defended most of all by the existence of a similar and even larger Soviet missile that could carry even more warheads. Now the priorities of both sides have been reversed. START I cut Soviet heavy missiles in half, and START II bans them; American multiwarhead missiles are also sharply limited and approved only in survivable submarines; the MX will be withdrawn. There are no audible complaints.

More deeply and broadly, there is now a consensus among strategists in and out of uniform that politics and strategic reality combine to make a stable strategic stalemate the best arrangement for both sides. In such a situation targeting for an unattainable victory becomes nonsensical. Both commanders and targeters dislike nonsense, so they begin to make more sensible plans. Economics also makes for moderation—both sides have other needs far more pressing than the maintenance of useless overkill.

On a quite different point, both sides can now handle strategic deployments and strategic planning in ways that take account of the political damage that is done when one side feels itself the immediate target of the other. Both President Bush and Secretary of Defense Cheney complained in early 1992 that Russian missiles were still aimed at the United States, and Yeltsin later gave comfort when he announced that all such missiles were being taken off alert. Can we suppose that Russian officials do not feel the same way about U.S. missiles? As long as there are missiles, they *can* be aimed at "the other side," but we believe that in reality both sides are determined not to make any bolt-from-the-blue attack, and confidence in this proposition is increased by closer relations between political and military leaders of the two countries. The possibility should not be excluded that each side could decide that the routine posture of its missiles should be that they are aimed at no target at all.

8. The U.S.-Russian reductions now in prospect should not be seen as the end of the road; in the long run Americans should work for still further reductions and improvements.

There is no higher priority for the reduction of nuclear danger than the orderly execution of all that is promised in START I and II and in the 1991 exchange of unilateral assurances on tactical warheads. Over the next few years the execution of these agreements and assurances should have operational priority, but the resulting level of 3,000 to 3,500 strategic warheads on each side should not be accepted as permanent. Over time, such acceptance could pin both sides into levels of expense that would be undesirable in themselves and destructive in their impact on the political relations between the two powers.

If we disregard the present size of the two great arsenals and simply ask ourselves what is the lowest level of strategic strength, measured in warheads, that would give both sides ample assurance both against nuclear attack and against the other side's breakout to any significant strategic superiority, we would not come out with the currently agreed range. That range reflects an understandable respect for existing habits of targeting, indeed for existing targets, that will not survive the changes already in prospect.

It may be better to examine the *long-run* prospects for lower warhead ceilings by a fresh start upward from zero, with ample safety factors. Assume that the United States will want to be able to hit both military and industrial targets, while keeping substantial forces in reserve and having insurance against losses from a surprise attack. The following table shows two alternative force levels for these purposes:

Military Targets	200	300
Industrial Targets	200	300
Reserve	100	150
Doubled for Insurance Against Surprise Attack	500	750
TOTAL	1,000	1,500

If the reductions now in prospect are carried out successfully, the United States and Russia may well be ready by the year 2000—and perhaps sooner—to go to one of these lower levels. Numbers like these might raise a question, in Moscow or Washington or both, about the comparative strength of British or French or Chinese forces. All three now appear to be headed toward numbers of strategic warheads in this same general range. But there is nothing immediately troubling here. If a continuing improvement in superpower nuclear relations permits the big two to agree on such reductions five or ten years from now, there may well emerge a parallel preference for reductions elsewhere. It may also become necessary, however, for Americans and Russians to accept forces in those countries that become relatively larger as time passes. Any resistance to such a relative change would be based more on habits of thought than on true national interest. Happily, recent events provide some evidence that nuclear moderation can be as contagious as nuclear competition was in the Cold War years.

To some arms controllers, even these reductions will seem like slow work. But just as it took time to build and deploy these enormous forces, so it will take time—though much less—to cut them back. Nor is 1,000 to 1,500 warheads the lowest level obtainable by the early twenty-first century. These numbers are put forward here only to make it clear that there is no good reason to accept the much higher targets of 1992 as the best that can ever be done.

Finally, it should be noted once more that reduction in warhead numbers is not the only means of nuclear restraint. The same broad objectives can also be served by reducing vulnerability, improving controls, avoiding destabilizing surprises, and making a broad attack on controlling and limiting weapons-grade material.

9. *The moderate and immediately practicable courses of action here recommended for the reduction of nuclear danger must also be held to the test that they should contribute to the prospect of further progress over the longer term.*

Some of the friends with whom we have discussed the preceding recommendations have asked us why we do not go further. Cannot the nuclear programs of some existing nuclear states be ended entirely? Can we not advocate a policy of no first use by anyone, especially the United States? Can we not envision numbers of warheads, even in the United States and Russia, that are well below the four-figure levels we have considered? Should we not, perhaps, revive the old notion of putting all nuclear weapons in the hands of an international agency? Could a properly arranged monopoly be operated by a selected government or governments on behalf of the UN? Should we not, in short, be more bold?

We have two answers to this set of questions. First, by the standards of the past, and also by what we know of the ways of nations, our proposals are more demanding than cautious. We ask for a sustained and genuine partnership of the nuclear superpowers in a shared program of national reductions, and of avoiding proliferation in the other countries of the former Soviet Union. We also propose that the United States call on all other countries to join in giving a new worldwide priority to the avoidance of further nuclear proliferation. We have argued that the nuclear moderation of every existing nuclear-weapon state will be critical to any such program. It is true that we have deliberately avoided detailed assignments of responsibility in these large undertakings, but we have done so out of respect for the reality that governments must make their own decisions. We do not think most governments will find our general recommendations undemanding.

Second, we accept the test that these short-term efforts must always be consistent with further progress toward the reduction of worldwide nuclear danger. We have examined all our proposals by this test, and we think they all make further steps easier, not harder. In particular, we think it is right to urge greater strength for international agencies, greater use of open formal treaties governing numbers, safeguards, and disclosure, and lower reliance on the threat of nuclear warfare.

10. American political leaders should set a new standard of openness in discussing these problems with other nations and with the American people.

It is not easy to understand many of the new realities explored in this book. Many of the lines of policy needed to deal with the new shape of nuclear danger do not fit well with much that Americans were used to only a few years ago. Most Americans recognize the great changes that have come with the end of the Cold War and the break-up of the Soviet Union. But when it comes to real choices, the subject of nuclear danger is a governmental concern, so leadership toward a new policy properly bought and paid for must continue to come from Washington. Recent presidents and Congresses have done much to reduce the level of nuclear danger in the world, but they have done less well in explaining and winning support for the new policy of partnership against nuclear danger that they have joined with foreign leaders to begin to create. Both recent achievements and future action will need the support of a more active policy of public explanation from American political leaders than we have ever had before on this subject.

More generally, it is time to replace the inherited distinction between those countries with nuclear weapons and those without by a wider assertion that all nations should be on the same side—*against* nuclear danger—whatever their present degree of reliance on nuclear weapons. This last proposition is so clear and strong that a steady respect for it is the best single guide to action for any country, both now and in the long run.

Index